A Trip to Cuba

Julia Ward Howe

Alpha Editions

This edition published in 2024

ISBN : 9789362091901

Design and Setting By
Alpha Editions
www.alphaedis.com
Email - info@alphaedis.com

As per information held with us this book is in Public Domain.
This book is a reproduction of an important historical work. Alpha Editions uses the best technology to reproduce historical work in the same manner it was first published to preserve its original nature. Any marks or number seen are left intentionally to preserve its true form.

Contents

CHAPTER I. THE DEPARTURE. .... - 1 -
CHAPTER II. NASSAU. .... - 5 -
CHAPTER III. FROM NASSAU TO CUBA. .... - 9 -
CHAPTER IV. THE HARBOR OF HAVANA. .... - 13 -
CHAPTER V. HAVANA. THE HOTELS. .... - 17 -
CHAPTER VI. HAVANA. YOUR BANKER. OUR CONSUL. THE FRIENDLY CUP OF TEA. .... - 20 -
CHAPTER VII. HAVANA—THE JESUIT COLLEGE. .... - 23 -
CHAPTER VIII. SAN ANTONIO DE LOS BAÑOS. .... - 26 -
CHAPTER IX. THE MORRO FORTRESS—THE UNIVERSITY OF HAVANA—THE BENEFICENZA. .... - 31 -
CHAPTER X. CAN GRANDE'S DEPARTURE.—THE DOMINICA.—LOTTERY-TICKETS. .... - 37 -
CHAPTER XI. COMPANY AT THE HOTEL.—SERVANTS.—OUR DRIVE.—DON PEPE. .... - 43 -
CHAPTER XII. MATANZAS. .... - 51 -
CHAPTER XIII. THE PASEO—THE PLAZA—DINING OUT. .... - 56 -
CHAPTER XIV. GAME-CHICKENS—DON RODRIGUEZ—DAY ON THE PLANTATION—DEPARTURE. .... - 60 -
CHAPTER XV. RETURN TO HAVANA—SAN ANTONIO AGAIN. .... - 67 -
CHAPTER XVI. SAN ANTONIO—CHURCH ON SUNDAY—THE NORTHER—THE S. FAMILY .... - 72 -
CHAPTER XVII. EDUCATION—LAST NIGHT IN SAN ANTONIO—FAREWELL. .... - 77 -
CHAPTER XVIII. SLAVERY—CUBAN SLAVE LAWS, INSTITUTIONS, ETC. .... - 81 -
CHAPTER XIX. FAREWELL! .... - 91 -

CHAPTER I.

THE DEPARTURE.

WHY one leaves home at all is a question that travellers are sure, sooner or later, to ask themselves,—I mean, pleasure-travellers. Home, where one has the "Transcript" every night, and the "Autocrat" every month, opera, theatre, circus, and good society, in constant rotation,—home, where everybody knows us, and the little good there is to know about us,—finally, home, as seen regretfully for the last time, with the gushing of long frozen friendships, the priceless kisses of children, and the last sad look at dear baby's pale face through the window-pane,—well, all this is left behind, and we review it as a dream, while the railroad-train hurries us along to the spot where we are to leave, not only this, but Winter, rude tyrant, with all our precious hostages in his grasp. Soon the swift motion lulls our brains into the accustomed muddle. We seem to be dragged along like a miserable thread pulled through the eye of an everlasting needle,—through and through, and never through,—while here and there, like painful knots, the *dépôts* stop us, the poor thread is arrested for a minute, and then the pulling begins again. Or, in another dream, we are like fugitives threading the gauntlet of the grim forests, while the ice-bound trees essay a charge of bayonets on either side; but, under the guidance of our fiery Mercury, we pass them as safely as ancient Priam passed the outposts of the Greeks,—and New York, hospitable as Achilles, receives us in its mighty tent. Here we await the "Karnak," the British Mail Company's new screw-steamer, bound for Havana, *viâ* Nassau. At length comes the welcome order to "be on board." We betake ourselves thither,—the anchor is weighed, the gun fired, and we take leave of our native land with a patriotic pang, which soon gives place to severer spasms.

I do not know why all celebrated people who write books of travels begin by describing their days of sea-sickness. Dickens, George Combe, Fanny Kemble, Mrs. Stowe, Miss Bremer, and many others, have opened in like manner their valuable remarks on foreign countries. While intending to avail myself of their privilege and example, I would nevertheless suggest, for those who may come after me, that the subject of sea-sickness should be embalmed in science, and enshrined in the crypt of some modern encyclopædia, so that future writers should refer to it only as the Pang Unspeakable, for which *vide* Ripley and Dana, vol., page. But, as I have already said, I shall speak of sea-sickness in a hurried and picturesque manner, as follows:—

Who are these that sit by the long dinner-table in the forward cabin, with a most unusual lack of interest in the bill of fare? Their eyes are closed, mostly, their cheeks are pale, their lips are quite bloodless, and to every offer of good cheer, their "No, thank you," is as faintly uttered as are marriage-vows by maiden lips. Can they be the same that, an hour ago, were so composed, so jovial, so full of dangerous defiance to the old man of the sea? The officer who carves the roast-beef offers at the same time a slice of fat;—this is too much; a panic runs through the ranks, and the rout is instantaneous and complete. The ghost of what each man was disappears through the trap-door of his state-room, and the hell which the theatre faintly pictures behind the scenes begins in good earnest.

For to what but to Dante's "Inferno" can we liken this steamboat-cabin, with its double row of pits, and its dismal captives? What are these sighs, groans, and despairing noises, but the *alti guai* rehearsed by the poet? Its fiends are the stewards who rouse us from our perpetual torpor with offers of food and praises of shadowy banquets,—"Nice mutton-chop, Sir? roast-turkey? plate of soup?" Cries of "No, no!" resound, and the wretched turn again, and groan. The Philanthropist has lost the movement of the age,—keeled up in an upper berth, convulsively embracing a blanket, what conservative more immovable than he? The Great Man of the party refrains from his large theories, which, like the circles made by the stone thrown into the water, begin somewhere and end nowhere. As we have said, he expounds himself no more, the significant forefinger is down, the eye no longer imprisons yours. But if you ask him how he does, he shakes himself as if, like Farinata,—

"avesse l'inferno in gran dispetto,"—

"he had a very contemptible opinion of hell."

Let me not forget to add, that it rains every day, that it blows every night, and that it rolls through the twenty-four hours till the whole world seems as if turned bottom upwards, clinging with its nails to chaos, and fearing to launch away. The Captain comes and says,—"It is true you have a nasty, short, chopping sea hereabouts; but you see, she is spinning away down South jolly!" And this is the Gulf-Stream!

But all things have an end, and most things have two. After the third day, a new development manifests itself. Various shapeless masses are carried upstairs and suffered to fall like snow-flakes on the deck, and to lie there in shivering heaps. From these larvæ gradually emerge features and voices,—the luncheon-bell at last stirs them with the thrill of returning life. They look up, they lean up, they exchange pensive smiles of recognition,—the Steward comes, no fiend this time, but a ministering angel; and lo! the strong man eats broth, and the weak woman clamors for pickled oysters. And so ends my description of our sea-sickness.

For, as for betraying the confidences of those sad days, as for telling how wofully untrue Professors of Temperance were to their principles, how the Apostle of Total Abstinence developed a brandy-flask, not altogether new, what unsuccessful tipplings were attempted in the desperation of nausea, and for what lady that stunning brandy-smasher was mixed,—as for such tales out of school, I would have you know that I am not the man to tell them.

Yet a portrait or so lingers in my mental repository;—let me throw them in, to close off the lot.

No. 1. A sober Bostonian in the next state-room, whose assiduity with his sea-sick wife reminds one of Cock-Robin, in the days when he sent Jenny Wren sops and wine. This person was last seen in a dressing-gown, square-cut night-cap, and odd slippers, dancing up and down the state-room floor with a cup of gruel, making wild passes with a spoon at an individual in a berth, who never got any of the contents. Item, the gruel, in a moment of excitement, finally ran in a stream upon the floor, and was wiped up by the Steward. Result not known, but disappointment is presumable.

No. 2. A stout lady, imprisoned by a board on a sofa nine inches wide, called by a facetious friend "The Coffin." She complains that her sides are tolerably battered in;—we hold our tongues, and think that the board, too, has had a hard time of it. Yet she is a jolly soul, laughing at her misfortunes, and chirruping to her baby. Her spirits keep up, even when her dinner won't keep down. Her favorite expressions are "Good George!" and "Oh, jolly!" She does not intend, she says, to lay in any dry goods in Cuba, but means to eat up all the good victuals she comes across. Though seen at present under unfavorable circumstances, she inspires confidence as to her final accomplishment of this result.

No. 3. A woman, said to be of a literary turn of mind, in the miserablest condition imaginable. Her clothes, flung at her by the Stewardess seem to have hit in some places, and missed in others. Her listless hands occasionally make an attempt to keep her draperies together, and to pull her hat on her head; but though the intention is evident, she accomplishes little by her motion. She is perpetually being lugged about by a stout steward, who knocks her head against both sides of the vessel, folds her up in the gangway, spreads her out on the deck, and takes her up-stairs, down-stairs, and in my lady's chamber, where, report says, he feeds her with a spoon, and comforts her with such philosophy as he is master of. N.B. This woman, upon the first change of weather, rose like a cork, dressed like a Christian, and toddled about the deck in the easiest manner, sipping her grog, and cutting sly jokes upon her late companions in misery,—is supposed by some to have been an impostor, and, when ill-treated, announced intentions of writing a book.

No. 4, my last, is only a sketch;—circumstances allowed no more. Can Grande, the great dog, has been got up out of the pit, where he worried the Stewardess and snapped at the friend who tried to pat him on the head. Everybody asks where he is. "Don't you see that heap of shawls yonder, lying in the sun, and heated up to about 212° Fahrenheit? That slouched hat on top marks the spot where his head should lie,—by treading cautiously in the opposite direction you may discover his feet. All between is perfectly passive and harmless. His chief food is pickles,—his only desire is rest. After all these years of controversy, after all these battles, bravely fought and nobly won, you might write with truth upon this moveless mound of woollens the pathetic words from Père la Chaise:—*Implora Pace*."

But no more at present, for land is in sight, and in my next you shall hear how we found it, and what we saw at Nassau.

CHAPTER II.

NASSAU.

NASSAU looked very green and pleasant to us after our voyage;—the eyes enjoy a little fresh provision after so long a course of salt food. The first view of land is little more than "the feeling of the thing,"—it is matter of faith, rather than of sight. You are shown a dark and distant line, near the horizon, without color or features. They say it is land, and you believe, it. But you come nearer and nearer,—you see first the green of vegetation, then the form of the trees,—the harbor at last opens its welcome arms,—the anchor is dropped,—the gun fired,—the steam snuffed out. Led by a thread of sunshine, you have walked the labyrinth of the waters, and all their gigantic dangers lie behind you.

We made Nassau at twelve o'clock, on the sixth day from our departure, counting the first as one. The earliest feature discernible was a group of tall cocoa-nut trees, with which the island is bounteously feathered;—the second was a group of negroes in a small boat, steering towards us with open-mouthed and white-toothed wonder. Nothing makes its simple impression upon the mind sophisticated by education. The negroes, as they came nearer, suggested only Christy's Minstrels, of whom they were a tolerably faithful imitation,—while the cocoa-nut trees transported us to the Boston in Ravel-time, and we strained our eyes to see the wonderful ape, Jocko, whose pathetic death, nightly repeated, used to cheat the credulous Bostonians of time, tears, and treasure. Despite the clumsiest management, the boat soon effected a junction with our gangway, allowing some nameless official to come on board, and to go through I know not what mysterious and indispensable formality. Other boats then came, like a shoal of little fishes around the carcass of a giant whale. There were many negroes, together with whites of every grade; and some of our number, leaning over the side, saw for the first time the raw material out of which Northern Humanitarians have spun so fine a skein of compassion and sympathy.

Now we who write, and they for whom we write, are all orthodox upon this mighty question. We have all made our confession of faith in private and in public; we all, on suitable occasions, walk up and apply the match to the keg of gunpowder which is to blow up the Union, but which, somehow, at the critical moment, fails to ignite. But you must allow us one heretical whisper,—very small and low. The negro of the North is an ideal negro; it is the negro refined by white culture, elevated by white blood, instructed even by white iniquity;—the negro among negroes is a coarse, grinning, flat-footed, thick-skulled creature, ugly as Caliban, lazy as the laziest of brutes, chiefly ambitious to be of no use to any in the world. View him as you will, his stock in trade is small;—he has but the tangible instincts of all creatures,—love of life, of ease, and of offspring. For all else, he must go to school to the white race, and his discipline must be long and laborious. Nassau, and all that we saw of it, suggested to us the unwelcome question whether compulsory labor be not better than none. But as a question I gladly leave it, and return to the simple narration of what befell.

There was a sort of eddy at the gangway of our steamer, made by the conflicting tides of those who wanted to come on board and of those who wanted to go on shore. We were among the number of the latter, but were stopped and held by the button by one of the former, while those more impatient or less sympathizing made their way to the small boats which waited below. The individual in question had come alongside in a handsome barge, rowed by a dozen stout blacks, in the undress uniform of the Zouaves. These men, well drilled and disciplined, seemed of a different sort from the sprawling, screaming creatures in the other boats, and their bright red caps and white tunics became them well. But he who now claimed my attention was of British birth and military profession. His face was ardent, his pantaloons were of white flannel, his expression of countenance was that of habitual discontent, but with a twinkle of geniality in the eye which redeemed the Grumbler from the usual tedium of his tribe. He accosted us as follows:—

"Go ashore? What for? To see something, eh? There's nothing to see; the island, isn't bigger than a nut-shell, and doesn't contain a single prospect.— Go ashore and get some dinner? There isn't anything to eat there.—Fruit? None to speak of; sour oranges and green bananas.—I went to market last Saturday, and bought one cabbage, one banana, and half a pig's head;— there's a market for you!—Fish? Oh, yes, if you like it.—Turtle? Yes, you can get the Gallipagos turtle; it makes tolerable soup, but has not the green fat, which, in *my* opinion, is the most important feature in turtle-soup.—Shops? You can't buy a pair of scissors on the island, nor a baby's bottle;—broke mine the other day, and tried to replace it; couldn't.—Society? There are lots of people to call upon you, and bore you to death with returning their visits."

At last the Major went below, and we broke away, and were duly conveyed to *terra firma*. It was Sunday, and late in the afternoon. The first glimpse certainly seemed to confirm the Major's disparaging statements. The town is small; the houses dingy and out of repair; the legend, that paint costs nothing, is not received here; and whatever may have been the original colors of the buildings, the climate has had its own way with them for many a day. The barracks are superior in finish to anything else we see. Government-House is a melancholy-looking *caserne*, surrounded by a piazza, the grounds being adorned with a most chunky and inhuman statue of Columbus. All the houses are surrounded by verandas, from which pale children and languid women in muslins look out, and incline us to ask what epidemic has visited the island and swept the rose from every cheek. They are a pallid race, the Nassauese, and retain little of the vigor of their English ancestry. One English trait they exhibit,—the hospitality which has passed into a proverb; another, perhaps,—the stanch adherence to the forms and doctrines of Episcopacy. We enter the principal church;—they are just lighting it for evening service; it is hung with candles, each burning in a clear glass shade. The walls and ceiling are white-washed, and contrast prettily with the dark timbering of the roof. We would gladly have staid to give thanks for our safe and prosperous voyage, but a black rain-cloud warns us homeward,—not, however, until we have received a kind invitation from one of the hospitable Islanders to return the next morning for a drive and breakfast.

Returning soon after sunrise to fulfil this promise, we encounter the barracks, and are tempted to look in and see the Sons of Darkness performing their evolutions. The morning drill is about half over. We peep in,—the Colonel, a lean Don Quixote on a leaner Rosinante, dashes up to us with a weak attempt at a canter; he courteously invites us to come in and see all that is to be seen, and lo! our friend the Major, quite gallant in his sword and scarlet jacket, is detailed for our service. The soldiers are black, and very black,— none of your dubious American shades, ranging from clear salmon to *café au lait* or even to *café noir*. These are your good, satisfactory, African sables, warranted not to change in the washing. Their Zouave costume is very becoming, with the Oriental turban, caftan, and loose trousers; and the Philosopher of our party remarks that the African requires costume, implying that the New Englander can stand alone, as can his clothes, in their black rigidity. The officers are white, and the Major very polite; he shows us the men, the arms, the kits, the quarters, and, having done all that he can do for us, relinquishes us with a gallant bow to our Host of the drive and breakfast.

The drive does something to retrieve the character of the island. The road is hard and even, overhung with glossy branches of strange trees bearing unknown fruits, and studded on each side with pleasant villas and with negro huts. There are lovely flowers everywhere, among which the Hibiscus, called South-Sea Rose, and the Oleander, are most frequent, and most brilliant. We see many tall groves of cocoa-nut, and cast longing glances towards the fruit, which little negroes, with surprising activity, attain and shake down. A sudden turn in the road discloses a lovely view of the bay, with its wonderful green waters, clear and bright as emerald;—there is a little beach, and boats lie about, and groups of negroes are laughing and chattering,—quoting stocks from the last fish-market, very likely. We purchase for half a dollar a bunch of bananas, for which Ford or Palmer would ask us ten dollars at least, and go rejoicing to our breakfast.

Our Host is a physician of the island, English by birth, and retaining his robust form and color in spite of a twenty-years' residence in the warm climate. He has a pleasant family of sons and daughters, all in health, but without a shade of pink in lips or cheeks. The breakfast consists of excellent fried fish, fine Southern hominy,—not the pebbly broken corn which our dealers impose under that name,—various hot cakes, tea and coffee, bananas, sapodillas, and if there be anything else not included in the present statement, let haste and want of time excuse the omission. The conversation runs a good deal on the hopes of increasing prosperity which the new mail-steamer opens to the eyes of the Nassauese. Invalids, they say, will do better there than in Cuba,—it is quieter, much cheaper, and the climate is milder. There will be a hotel very soon, where no attention will be spared, etc., etc. The Government will afford every facility, etc., etc. It seemed indeed a friendly little place, with delicious air and sky, and a good, reasonable, decent, English tone about it. Expenses moderate, ye fathers of encroaching families. Negroes abundant and natural, ye students of ethnological possibilities. Officers in red jackets, you young ladies,—young ones, some of them. Why wouldn't you all try it, especially as the Captain of the "Karnak" is an excellent sailor, and the kindest and manliest of conductors?

CHAPTER III.

FROM NASSAU TO CUBA.

THE breakfast being over, we recall the Captain's parting admonition to be on board by ten o'clock, with the significant gesture and roll of the eye which clearly express that England expects every passenger to do his duty. Now we know very well that the "Karnak" is not likely to weigh anchor before twelve, at the soonest, but we dare not for our lives disobey the Captain. So, passing by yards filled with the huge Bahama sponges, piles of wreck-timber, fishing-boats with strange fishes, red, yellow, blue, and white, and tubs of aldermanic turtle, we attain the shore, and presently, the steamer. Here we find a large deputation of the towns-people taking passage with us for a pleasure excursion to Havana. The greater number are ladies and children. They come fluttering on board, poor things, like butterflies, in gauzy dresses, hats, and feathers, according to the custom of their country; one gentleman takes four little daughters with him for a holiday. We ask ourselves whether they know what an ugly beast the Gulf-Stream is, that they affront him in such light armor. "Good heavens! how sick they will be!" we exclaim; while they eye us askance, in our winter trim, and pronounce us slow, and old fogies. With all the rashness of youth, they attack the luncheon-table. So boisterous a popping of corks was never heard in all our boisterous passage;—there is a chorus, too, of merry tongues and shrill laughter. But we get fairly out to sea, where the wind, an adverse one, is waiting for us, and at that gay table there is silence, followed by a rush and disappearance. The worst cases are hurried out of sight, and going above, we find the disabled lying in groups about the deck, the feather-hats discarded, the muslins crumpled, and we, the old fogies, going to cover the fallen with shawls and blankets, to speak words of consolation, and to implore the sufferers not to cure themselves with brandy, soda-water, claret, and wine-bitters, in quick succession,—which they, nevertheless, do, and consequently are no better that day, nor the next.

But I am forgetting to chronicle a touching parting interview with the Major, the last thing remembered in Nassau, and of course the last to be forgotten anywhere. Our concluding words might best be recorded in the form of a catechism of short questions and answers, to wit:—

"How long did the Major expect to stay in Nassau?"

"About six months."

"How long would he stay, if he had his own way?"

"Not one!"

"What did he come for, then?"

"Oh, you buy into a nigger regiment for promotion."

These were the most important facts elicited by cross-examination. At last we shook hands warmly, promising to meet again somewhere, and the crimson-lined barge with the black Zouaves carried him away. In humbler equipages depart the many black women who have visited the steamer, some for amusement, some to sell the beautiful shell-work made on the island. These may be termed, in general, as ugly a set of wenches as one could wish not to see. They all wear palm-leaf hats stuck on their heads without strings or ribbons, and their clothes are so ill-made that you cannot help thinking that each has borrowed somebody else's dress, until you see that the ill-fitting garments are the rule, not the exception.

But neither youth nor sea-sickness lasts forever. The forces of nature rally on the second day, and the few who have taken no remedies recover the use of their tongues and some of their faculties. From these I gather what I shall here impart as

SERIOUS VIEWS OF THE BAHAMAS.

The principal exports of these favored islands are fruits, sponges, molasses, and sugar. Their imports include most of the necessaries of life, which come to them oftenest in the form of wrecks, by which they obtain them at a small fraction of the original cost and value. For this resource they are indebted to the famous Bahama Banks, which to their way of thinking are institutions as important as the Bank of England itself. These banks stand them in a handsome annual income, and facilitate large discounts and transfers of property not contemplated by the original possessors. One supposes that somebody must suffer by these forced sales of large cargoes at prices ruinous to commerce,—but *who* suffers is a point not easy to ascertain. There seems to be a good, comfortable understanding all round. The Owners say, "Go ahead, and don't bother yourself,—she's insured." The Captain has got his ship aground in shoal water where she can't sink, and no harm done. The friendly wreckers are close at hand to haul the cargo ashore. The Underwriter of the insurance company has shut his eyes and opened his mouth to receive a plum, which, being a good large one, will not let him speak. And so the matter providentially comes to pass, and "enterprises of great pith and moment" oftenest get no further than the Bahamas.

Nassau produces neither hay nor corn,—these, together with butter, flour, and tea, being brought chiefly from the United States. Politics, of course, it has none. As to laws, the colonial system certainly needs propping up,—for under its action a man may lead so shameless a life of immorality as to compel his wife to leave him, and yet not be held responsible for her support and that of the children she has borne him. The principal points of interest are, first, the garrison,—secondly, Government-House, with an occasional ball there,—and, third, one's next-door neighbor, and his or her doings. The principal event in the memory of the citizens seems to be a certain most desirable wreck, in consequence of which, a diamond card-case, worth fifteen hundred dollars, was sold for an eighth part of that sum, and laces, whose current price ranges from thirty to forty dollars a yard, were purchased at will for seventy-five cents. That was a wreck worth having! say the Nassauese. The price of milk ranges from eighteen to twenty-five cents a quart;—think of that, ye New England housekeepers! That precious article, the pudding, is nearly unknown in the Nassauese economy; nor is pie-crust so short as it might be, owing to the enormous price of butter, which has been known to attain the sum of one dollar per pound. Eggs are quoted at prices not commendable for large families with small means. On the other hand, fruits, vegetables, and sugar-cane are abundant.

The Nassauese, on the whole, seem to be a kind-hearted and friendly set of people, partly English, partly Southern in character, but with rather a predominance of the latter ingredient in their composition. Their women resemble the women of our own Southern States, but seem simpler and more domestic in their habits,—while the men would make tolerable Yankees, but would scarcely support President Buchanan, the Kansas question, or the Filibustero movement. Physically, the race suffers and degenerates under the influence of the warm climate. Cases of pulmonary disease, asthma, and neuralgia are of frequent occurrence, and cold is considered as curative to them as heat is to us. The diet, too, is not that "giant ox-beef" which the Saxon race requires. Meat is rare and tough, unless brought from the States at high cost. We were forced to the conclusion that no genuine English life can be supported upon a *régime* of fish and fruit,—or, in other words, no beef, no Bull, but a very different sort of John, lantern-jawed, leather-skinned, and of a thirsty complexion. It occurred to us, furthermore, that it is a dolorous thing to live on a lonely little island, tied up like a wart on the face of civilization,—no healthful stream of life coming and going from the great body of the main land,—the same moral air to be breathed over and over again, without renewal,—the same social elements turned and returned in one tiresome kaleidoscope. Wherefore rejoice, ye Continentals, and be thankful, and visit the Nassauese, bringing beef, butter, and beauty,—bringing a few French muslins, to replace the coarse English fabrics, and buxom Irish girls to outwork the idle negro women,—bringing new books, newspapers, and periodicals,—bringing the Yankee lecturer, all expenses paid, and his drink found him. All these good things, and more, the States have for the Nassauese, of whom we must now take leave, for all hands have been piped on deck.

We have jolted for three weary days over the roughest of ocean-highways, and Cuba, nay, Havana, is in sight. The worst cases are up, and begin to talk about their sea-legs, now that the occasion for them is at an end. Sobrina, the chief wit of our party, who would eat sour-sop, sapodilla, orange, banana, cocoa-nut, and sugar-cane at Nassau, and who has lived upon toddy of twenty-cocktail power ever since,—even she is seen, clothed and in her right mind, sitting at the feet of the Prophet she loves, and going through the shawl-and-umbrella exercise. And here is the Morro Castle, which guards the entrance of the harbor,—here go the signals, answering to our own. Here comes the man with the speaking-trumpet, who, understanding no English, yells out to our captain, who understands no Spanish. The following is a free rendering of their conversation:—

"Any Americans on board?"

"Yes, thank Heaven, plenty."

"How many are Filibusteros?"

"All of them."

"Bad luck to them, then!"

"The same to you!"

"*Caramba*," says the Spaniard.

"—— ——," says the Englishman.

And so the forms of diplomacy are fulfilled; and of Havana, more in my next.

CHAPTER IV.

THE HARBOR OF HAVANA.

AS we have said, there were some official mysteries connected with the arrival of our steamer in Nassau; but these did not compare with the visitations experienced in Havana. As soon as we had dropped anchor, a swarm of dark creatures came on board, with gloomy brows, mulish noses, and suspicious eyes. This application of Spanish flies proves irritating to the good-natured Captain, and uncomfortable to all of us. All possible documents are produced for their satisfaction,—bill of lading, bill of health, and so on. Still they persevere in tormenting the whole ship's crew, and regard us, when we pass, with all the hatred of race in their rayless eyes. "Is it a crime," we are disposed to ask, "to have a fair Saxon skin, blue eyes, and red blood?" Truly, one would seem to think so; and the first glance at this historical race makes clear to us the Inquisition, the Conquest of Granada, and the ancient butcheries of Alva and Pizarro.

As Havana is an unco uncertain place for accommodations, we do not go on shore, the first night, but, standing close beside the bulwarks, feel a benevolent pleasure in seeing our late companions swallowed and carried off like tidbits by the voracious boatmen below, who squabble first for them and then with them, and so gradually disappear in the darkness. On board the "Karnak" harmony reigns serene. The custom-house wretches are gone, and we are, on the whole, glad we did not murder them. Our little party enjoys tea and bread-and-butter together for the last time. After so many mutual experiences of good and evil, the catguts about our tough old hearts are loosened, and discourse the pleasant music of Friendship. An hour later, I creep up to the higher deck, to have a look-out forward, where the sailors are playing leap-frog and dancing fore-and-afters. I have a genuine love of such common sights, and am quite absorbed by the good fun before me, when a solemn voice sounds at my left, and looking round, I perceive Can Grande, who has come up to explain to me the philosophy of the sailor's dances, and to unfold his theory of amusements, as far as the narrow area of one little brain (mine, not his) will permit. His monologue, and its interruptions, ran very much as follows:—

I.—This is a pleasant sight, isn't it?

Can Grande.—It has a certain interest, as exhibiting the inborn ideal tendency of the human race;—no tribe of people so wretched, so poor, or so infamous as to dispense with amusement, in some form or other.

Voice from below.—Play up, Cook! That's but a slow jig ye're fluting away at.

Can Grande.—I went once to the Five Points of New York, with a police-officer and two philanthropists;—our object was to investigate that lowest phase of social existence.——

Bang, whang, go the wrestlers below, with loud shouts and laughter. I give them one eye and ear,—Can Grande has me by the other.

Can Grande.—I went into one of their miserable dance-saloons. I saw there the vilest of men and the vilest of women, meeting with the worst intentions; but even for this they had the fiddle, music and dancing. Without this little crowning of something higher, their degradation would have been intolerable to themselves and to each other.——

Here the man who gave the back in leap-frog suddenly went down in the middle of the leap, bringing with him the other who, rolling on the deck, caught the traitor by the hair, and pommeled him to his heart's content. I ventured to laugh, and exclaim, "Did you see that?"

Can Grande.—Yes; that is very common.—At that dance of death, every wretched woman had such poor adornment as her circumstances allowed,—a collar, a tawdry ribbon, a glaring false jewel, her very rags disposed with the greater decency of the finer sex,—a little effort at beauty, a sense of it. The good God puts it there;—He does not allow the poorest, the lowest of his human children the thoughtless indifference of brutes.——

And there was the beautiful tropical sky above, starry, soft, and velvet-deep,—the placid waters all around, and at my side the Man who is to speak no more in public, but whose words in private have still the old thrill, the old power to shake the heart and bring the good thoughts uppermost. I put my hand in his, and we descended the companion-way together, and left the foolish sailors to their play.

But now, on the after-deck, the Captain, entreated and in nowise unwilling, takes down his violin, and with pleasant touch gives us the dear old airs, "Home, Sweet Home," "Annie Laurie," and so on, and we accompany him with voices toned down by the quiet of the scene around. He plays too, with a musing look, the merry tune to which his little daughter dances, in the English dancing-school, hundreds of leagues away. Good-night, at last, and make the most of it. Coolness and quiet on the water to-night, and heat and mosquitoes, howling of dogs and chattering of negroes to-morrow night, in Havana.

The next morning allowed us to accomplish our transit to the desired land of Havana. We pass the Custom-house, where an official in a cage, with eyes of most oily sweetness, and tongue, no doubt, to match, pockets our gold, and imparts in return a governmental permission to inhabit the island of Cuba for the space of one calendar month. We go trailing through the market, where we buy peeled oranges, and through the streets, where we eat them, seen and recognized afar as Yankees by our hats, bonnets, and other features. We stop at the Café Dominica, and refresh with coffee and buttered rolls, for we have still a drive of three miles to accomplish before breakfast. All the hotels in Havana are full, and more than full. Woolcut, of the Cerro, three miles from the gates, is the only landlord who will take us in; so he seizes us fairly by the neck, bundles us into an omnibus, swears that his hotel is but two miles distant, smiles archly when we find the two miles long, brings us where he wants to have us, the Spaniards in the omnibus puffing and staring at the ladies all the way. Finally, we arrive at his hotel, glad to be somewhere, but hot, tired, hungry, and not in raptures with our first experience of tropical life.

It must be confessed that our long-tried energies fall somewhat flat on the quiet of Woolcut's. We look round, and behold one long room with marble floor, with two large doors, not windows, opening in front upon the piazza and the street, and other openings into a large court behind, surrounded by small, dark bedrooms. The large room is furnished with two dilapidated cane sofas, a few chairs, a small table, and three or four indifferent prints, which we have ample time to study. For company, we see a stray New York or Philadelphia family, a superannuated Mexican who smiles and bows to everybody, and some dozen of those undistinguishable individuals whom we class together as Yankees, and who, taking the map from Maine to Georgia, might as well come from one place as another, the Southerner being as like the Northerner as a dried pea is to a green pea. The ladies begin to hang their heads, and question a little:—"What are we to do here? and where is the perfectly delightful Havana you told us of?" Answer:—"There is nothing whatever to do here, at this hour of the day, but to undress and go to sleep;— the heat will not let you stir, the glare will not let you write or read. Go to bed; dinner is at four; and after that, we will make an effort to find the Havana of the poetical and Gan Eden people, praying Heaven it may not have its only existence in their brains."

Still, the pretty ones do not brighten. They walk up and down, eyeing askance the quiet boarders who look so contented over their children and worsted-work, and wondering in what part of the world they have taken the precaution to leave their souls. Unpacking is then begun, with rather a flinging of the things about, interspersed with little peppery hints as to discomfort and dulness, and dejected stage-sighs, intended for hearing. But this cannot go on,—the thermometer is at 78° in the shade,—an intense and contagious stillness reigns through the house,—some good genius waves a bunch of poppies near those little fretful faces, for which a frown is rather heavy artillery. The balmy breath of sleep blows off the lightly-traced furrows, and after a dreamy hour or two all is bright, smooth, and freshly dressed, as a husband could wish it. The dinner proves not intolerable, and after it we sit on the piazza. A refreshing breeze springs up, and presently the tide of the afternoon drive sets in from the city. The *volantes* dash by, with silver-studded harnesses, and postilions black and booted; within sit the pretty Señoritas, in twos and threes. They are attired mostly in muslins, with bare necks and arms; bonnets they know not,—their heads are dressed with flowers, or with jewelled pins. Their faces are whitened, we know, with powder, but in the distance the effect is pleasing. Their dark eyes are vigilant; they know a lover when they see him. But there is no twilight in these parts, and the curtain of the dark falls upon the scene as suddenly as the screen of the theatre upon the *dénouement* of the tragedy. Then comes a cup of truly infernal tea, the mastication of a stale roll, with butter, also stale,—then, more sitting on the piazza,—then, retirement, and a wild hunt after mosquitoes,—and so ends the first day at Woolcut's, on the Cerro.

CHAPTER V.

HAVANA. THE HOTELS.

"SHALL I not take mine ease in mine inn?" Yes, truly, if you can get it, Jack Falstaff; but it is one thing to pay for comfort, and another thing to have it. You certainly pay for it, in Havana; for the $3 or $3.50 *per diem*, which is your simplest hotel-charge there, should, in any civilized part of the world, give you a creditable apartment, clean linen, and all reasonable diet. What it does give, the travelling public may like to learn.

Can Grande has left Woolcut's. The first dinner did not please him,—the cup of tea, with only bread, exasperated,—and the second breakfast, greasy, peppery, and incongruous, finished his disgust; so he asked for his bill, packed his trunk, called the hotel detestable, and went.

Now he was right enough in this; the house is detestable;—but as all houses of entertainment throughout the country are about equally so, it is scarcely fair to complain of one. I shall not fear to be more inclusive in my statement, and to affirm that in no part of the world does one get so little comfort for so much money as on the Island of Cuba. To wit: an early cup of black coffee, oftenest very bad; bread not to be had without an extra sputtering of Spanish, and darkening of the countenance;—to wit, a breakfast between nine and ten, invariably consisting of fish, rice, beefsteak, fried plantains, salt cod with tomatoes, stewed tripe and onions, indifferent claret, and an after-cup of coffee or green tea;—to wit, a dinner at three or four, of which the inventory varieth not,—to wit, a plate of soup, roast beef, tough turkeys and chickens, tolerable ham, nameless stews, cayota, plantains, salad, sweet potatoes; and for dessert, a spoonful each of West India preserve,—invariably the kind you do not like,—oranges, bananas, and another cup of coffee;—to wit, tea of the sort already described;—to wit, attendance and non-attendance of negro and half-breed waiters, who mostly speak no English, and neither know nor care what you want;—to wit, a room whose windows, reaching from floor to ceiling, inclose no glass, and are defended from the public by iron rails, and from the outer air, at desire, by clumsy wooden shutters, which are closed only when it rains;—to wit, a bed with a mosquito-netting;—to wit, a towel and a pint of water, for all ablutions. This is the sum of your comforts as to quantity; but as to their quality, experience alone can enlighten you.

Taking pity on my exile at the Cerro, Can Grande and his party invite me to come and spend a day at their hotel, of higher reputation, and situated in the centre of things. I go;—the breakfast, to my surprise, is just like Woolcut's; the dinner *idem*, but rather harder to get; preserves for tea, and two towels daily, instead of one, seem to constitute the chief advantages of this establishment. Domestic linens, too, are fairer than elsewhere; but when you have got your ideas of cleanliness down to the Cuban standard, a shade or two either way makes no material difference.

Can Grande comes and goes; for stay in the hotel, behind those prison-gratings, he cannot. He goes to the market and comes back, goes to the Jesuit College and comes back, goes to the Banker's and gets money. In his encounters with the sun he is like a prize-fighter coming up to time. Every round finds him weaker and weaker, still his pluck is first-rate, and he goes at it again. It is not until three, P. M., that he wrings out his dripping pocket-handkerchief, slouches his hat over his brows, and gives in as dead-beat.

They of the lovely sex meanwhile undergo, with what patience they may, an Oriental imprisonment. In the public street they must on no account set foot. The Creole and Spanish women are born and bred to this, and the hardiest American or English woman will scarcely venture out a second time without the severe escort of husband or brother. These relatives are, accordingly, in great demand. In the thrifty North, Man is considered an incumbrance from breakfast to dinner,—and the sooner he is fed and got out of the way in the morning, the better the work of the household goes on. If the master of the house return at an unseasonable hour, he is held to an excuse, and must prove a headache, or other suitable indisposition. In Havana, on the contrary, the American woman suddenly becomes very fond of her husband:—"he must not leave her at home alone; where does he go? she will go with him; when will he come back? Remember, now, she will expect him." The secret of all this is that she cannot go out without him. The other Angel of deliverance is the *volante*, with its tireless horses and *calesero*, who seems fitted and screwed to the saddle, which he never leaves. He does not even turn his head for orders. His senses are in the back of his head, or wherever his Mistress pleases. "*José, Calle de la Muralla, esquina á los oficios*,"—and the black machine moves on, without look, word, or sign of intelligence. In New York, your Irish coachman grins approval of your order; and even an English flunkey may touch his hat and say, "Yes, Mum." But in the Cuban negro of service, dumbness is the complement of darkness. You speak, and the patient right hand pulls the strap that leads the off horse, while the other gathers up the reins of the nigh, and the horses, their tails tightly braided and deprived of all movement, seem as mechanical as the driver. Happy are the ladies at the hotel who have a perpetual *volante* at their service! for they dress in their best clothes three times a day, and do not soil them by contact with the dusty street. They drive before breakfast, and shop before dinner, and after dinner go to flirt their fans and refresh their robes on the Paseo, where the fashions drive. At twilight, they stop at friendly doors and pay visits, or at the entrance of the *café*, where ices are brought out to them. At eight o'clock they go to the Plaza, and hear the band play, sitting in the *volante*; and at ten they come home without fatigue, having all day taken excellent care of Number One, beyond which their arithmetic does not extend. "I and my *volante*" is like Cardinal Wolsey's "*Ego et Rex meus*."

As for those who have no *volantes*, modesty becomes them, and quietness of dress and demeanor. They get a little walk before breakfast, and stay at home all day, or ride in an omnibus, which is perhaps worse;—they pay a visit now and then in a hired carriage, the bargain being made with difficulty;—they look a good deal through the bars of the windows, and remember the free North, and would, perhaps, envy the *volante*-commanding women, did not dreadful Moses forbid.

One alleviation of the tedium of hotel-life in the city is the almost daily visit of the young man from the dry-goods' shop, who brings samples of lawns, linen dresses, piña handkerchiefs, and fans of all prices, from two to seventy-five dollars. The ladies cluster like bees around these flowery goods, and, after some hours of bargaining, disputing, and purchasing, the vendor pockets the golden honey, and marches off. As dressmakers in Havana are scarce, dear, and bad, our fair friends at the hotel make up these dresses mostly themselves, and astonish their little world every day by appearing in new attire. "How extravagant!" you say. They reply, "Oh! it cost nothing for the making; I made it myself." But we remember to have heard somewhere that "Time is Money." At four in the afternoon, a negress visits in turn every bedroom, sweeps out the mosquitoes from the curtains with a feather-brush, and lets down the mosquito-net, which she tucks in around the bed. After this, do not meddle with your bed until it is time to get into it; then put the light away, open the net cautiously, enter with a dexterous swing, and close up immediately, leaving no smallest opening to help them after. In this mosquito-net you live, move, and have your being until morning; and should you venture to pull it aside, even for an hour, you will appall your friends, next day, with a face which suggests the early stages of small-pox, or the spotted fever.

The valuable information I have now communicated is the sum of what I learned in that one day at Mrs. Almy's; and though our party speedily removed thither, I doubt whether I shall be able to add to it anything of importance.

CHAPTER VI.

HAVANA. YOUR BANKER. OUR CONSUL. THE FRIENDLY CUP OF TEA.

ONE is apt to arrive in Havana with a heart elated by the prospect of such kindnesses and hospitalities as are poetically supposed to be the perquisite of travellers. You count over your letters as so many treasures; you regard the unknown houses you pass as places of deposit for the new acquaintances and delightful friendships which await you. In England, say you, each of these letters would represent a pleasant family-mansion thrown open to your view,—a social breakfast,—a dinner of London wits,—a box at the opera,—or the visit of a Lord, whose perfect carriage and livery astonish the quiet street in which you lodge, and whose good taste and good manners should, one thinks, prove contagious, at once soothing and shaming the fretful Yankee conceit. But your Cuban letters, like fairy money, soon turn to withered leaves in your possession, and, having delivered two or three of them, you employ the others more advantageously, as shaving-paper, or for the lighting of cigars, or any other useful purpose.

Your Banker, of course, stands first upon the list,—and to him accordingly, with a beaming countenance, you present yourself. For him you have a special letter of recommendation, and however others may fail, you consider him as sure as the trump of the deal at whist. But why, alas, should people, who have gone through the necessary disappointments of life, prepare for themselves others, which may be avoided? Listen and learn. At the first visit, your Banker is tolerably glad to see you,—he discounts your modest letter of credit, and pockets his two and a half *per cent*, with the best grace imaginable. If he wishes to be very civil, he offers you a seat, offers you a cigar, and mumbles in an indistinct tone that he will be happy to serve you in any way. You call again and again, keeping yourself before his favorable remembrance,—always the same seat, the same cigar, the same desire to serve you, carefully repressed, and prevented from breaking out into any overt demonstration of good-will. At last, emboldened by the brilliant accounts of former tourists and the successes of your friends, you suggest that you would like to see a plantation,—you only ask for one,—would he give you a letter, etc., etc.? He assumes an abstracted air, wonders if he knows anybody who has a plantation,—the fact being that he scarcely knows anybody who has not one. Finally, he will try,—call again, and he will let you know. You call again,—"Next week," he says. You call after that interval,—"Next week," again, is all you get. Now, if you are a thorough-bred man, you can afford to quarrel with your Banker; so you say, "Next week,—why not next year?"—make a very decided snatch at your hat, and wish him a very long "good-morning." But if you are a Snob and afraid, you take his neglect quietly enough, and will boast, when you go home, of his polite attentions to yourself and family, when on the Island of Cuba.

Our Consul is the next post in the weary journey of your hopes, and to him, with such assurance as you have left, you now betake yourself. Touching him personally I have nothing to say. I will only remark, in general, that the traveller who can find, in any part of the world, an American Consul not disabled from all service by ill-health, want of means, ignorance of foreign languages, or unpleasant relations with the representatives of foreign powers,—that traveller, we say, should go in search of the sea-serpent, and the passage of the North Pole, for he has proved himself able to find what, to every one but him, is undiscoverable.

But who, setting these aside, is to show you any attention? Who will lift you from the wayside, and set you upon his own horse, or in his own *volante*, pouring oil and wine upon your wounded feelings? Ah! the breed of the good Samaritan is never allowed to become extinct in this world, where so much is left for it to do.

A kind and hospitable American family, long resident in Havana, takes us up at last. They call upon us, and we lift up our heads; they take us out in their carriage, and we step in with a little familiar flounce, intended to show that we are used to such things; finally, they invite us to a friendly cup of tea,—all the hotel knows it,—we have tarried at home in the shade long enough. Now, people have begun to find us out,—*we are going out to tea*!

How pleasant the tea-table was, how good the tea, how more than good the bread-and-butter and plum-cake, how quaint the house of Spanish construction, all open to the air, adorned with flowers like a temple, fresh and fragrant, and with no weary upholstery to sit heavy on the sight, how genial and prolonged the talk, how reluctant the separation,—imagine it, ye who sing the songs of home in a strange land. And ye who cannot imagine, forgo the pleasure, for I shall tell you no more about it. I will not, I, give names, to make good-natured people regret the hospitality they have afforded. If they have entertained unawares angels and correspondents of the press, (I use the two terms as synonymous,) they shall not be made aware of it by the sacrifice of their domestic privacy. All celebrated people do this, and that we do it not answers for our obscurity.

The cup of tea proves the precursor of many kind services and pleasant hours. Our new friends assist us to a deal of sight-seeing, and introduce us to cathedral, college, and garden. We walk out with them at sunrise and at sunset, and sit under the stately trees, and think it almost strange to be at home with people of our own race and our own way of thinking, so far from the home-surroundings. For the gardens, they may chiefly be described as triumphs of Nature over Art,—our New England horticulture being, on the contrary, the triumph of Art over Nature, after a hard-fought battle. Here, the avenues of palm and cocoa are magnificent, and the flowers new to us, and very brilliant. But pruning and weeding out are hard tasks for Creole natures, with only negroes to help them. There is for the most part a great overgrowth and overrunning of the least desirable elements, a general air of slovenliness and unthrift. In all artificial arrangements decay seems imminent, and the want of idea in the laying out of grounds is a striking feature. In Italian villas, the feeling of the Beautiful, which has produced a race of artists, is everywhere manifest,—everywhere are beautiful forms and picturesque effects. Even the ruins of Rome seem to be held together by this fine bond. No stone dares to drop, no arch to moulder, but with an exquisite and touching grace. And the weeds, oh! the weeds that hang their little pennon on the Coliseum, how graciously do they float, as if they said,—"Breathe softly, lest this crumbling vision of the Past go down before the rude touch of the modern world!" And so one treads lightly, and speaks in hushed accents; lest, in the brilliant Southern noon, one should wake the sleeping heart of Rome to the agony of her slow extinction.

But what is all this? We are dreaming of Rome,—and this is Cuba, where the spirit of Art has never been, and where it could not pass without sweeping out from houses, churches, gardens, and brains, such trash as has rarely been seen and endured elsewhere. They show us, for example, some mutilated statues in the ruins of what is called the Bishop's Garden. Why, the elements did a righteous work, when they effaced the outlines of these coarse and trivial shapes, unworthy even the poor marble on which they were imposed. Turning from these, however, we find lovely things enough to rebuke this savage mood of criticism. The palm-trees are unapproachable in beauty,—they stand in rows like Ionic columns, straight, strong, and regular, with their plumed capitals. They talk solemnly of the Pyramids and the Desert, whose legends have been whispered to them by the winds that cross the ocean, freighted with the thoughts of God. Then, these huge white lilies, deep as goblets, from which one drinks fragrance, and never exhausts,—these thousand unknown jewels of the tropics. Here is a large tank, whose waters are covered with the leaves and flowers of beautiful aquatic plants, whose Latin names are of no possible consequence to anybody. Here, in the very heart of the garden, is a rustic lodge, curtained with trailing vines. Birds in cages are hung about it, and a sweet voice, singing within, tells us that the lodge is the cage of a yet more costly bird. We stop to listen, and the branches of the trees seem to droop more closely about us, the twilight lays its cool, soft touch upon our heated foreheads, and we whisper,—"Peace to his soul!" as we leave the precincts of the Bishop's Garden.

CHAPTER VII.

HAVANA—THE JESUIT COLLEGE.

THE gentlemen of our party go one day to visit the Jesuit College in Havana, yclept "*Universidad de Belen.*" The ladies, weary of dry goods, manifest some disposition to accompany them. This is at once frowned down by the unfairer sex, and Can Grande, appealed to by the other side, shakes his shoulders, and replies, "No, you are only miserable women, and cannot be admitted into any Jesuit establishment whatever." And so the male deputation departs with elation, and returns with airs of superior opportunity, and is more insufferable than ever at dinner, and thereafter.

They of the feminine faction, on the other hand, consult with more direct authorities, and discover that the doors of Belen are in nowise closed to them, and that everything within those doors is quite at their disposition, saving and excepting the sleeping-apartments of the Jesuit fathers,—to which, even in thought, they would on no account draw near. And so they went and saw Belen, whereof one of them relates as follows.

The building is spacious, inclosing a hollow square, and with numerous galleries, like European cloisters, where the youth walk, study, and play. We were shown up-stairs, into a pleasant reception-room, where two priests soon waited on us. One of these, Padre Doyaguez, seemed to be the decoy-duck of the establishment, and soon fastened upon one of our party, whose Protestant tone of countenance had probably caught his attention. Was she a Protestant? Oh, no!—not with that intelligent physiognomy!—not with that talent! What was her name? Julia (pronounced *H*ulia). Hulia was a Roman name, a Catholic name; he had never heard of a Hulia who was a Protestant;—very strange, it seemed to him, that a Hulia could hold to such unreasonable ideas. The other priest, Padre Lluc, meanwhile followed with sweet, quiet eyes, whose silent looks had more persuasion in them than all the innocent cajoleries of the elder man. Padre Doyaguez was a man eminently qualified to deal with the sex in general,—a coaxing voice, a pair of vivacious eyes whose cunning was not unpleasing, tireless good-humor and perseverance, and a savor of sincerity. Padre Lluc was the sort of man that one recalls in quiet moments with a throb of sympathy,—the earnest eyes, the clear brow, the sonorous voice. One thinks of him, and hopes that he is satisfied,—that cruel longing and more cruel doubt shall never spring up in that capacious heart, divorcing his affections and convictions from the system to which his life is irrevocably wedded. No, keep still, Padre Lluc! think ever as you think now, lest the faith that seems a fortress should prove a prison, the mother a step-dame,—lest the high, chivalrous spirit, incapable of a safe desertion, should immolate truth or itself on the altar of consistency.

Between those two advocates of Catholicity, Hulia Protestante walks slowly through the halls of the University. She sees first a Cabinet of Natural History, including minerals, shells, fossils, and insects, all well-arranged, and constituting a very respectable beginning. Padre Lluc says some good words on the importance of scientific education. Padre Doyaguez laughs at the ladies' hoops, which he calls Malakoffs, as they crowd through the doorways and among the glass cases; he repeats occasionally, "*Hulia Protestante?*" in a tone of mock astonishment, and receives for answer, "*Si, Hulia Protestante.*" Then comes a very creditable array of scientific apparatus,—not of the order employed by the judges of Galileo,—electric and galvanic batteries, an orrery, and many things beside. The Library interests us more, with some luxurious Classics, a superb Dante, and a prison-cage of forbidden works, of which Padre Lluc certainly has the key. Among these were fine editions of Rousseau and Voltaire, which appeared to be intended for use; and we could imagine a solitary student, dark-eyed and pale, exploring their depths at midnight with a stolen candle, and endeavoring, with self-torment, to reconcile the intolerance of his doctrine with the charities of his heart. We imagine such an one lost in the philosophy and sentiment of the "Nouvelle Héloïse," and suddenly summoned by the convent-bell to the droning of the Mass, the mockery of Holy Water, the fable of the Real Presence. Such contrasts might be strange and dangerous. No, no, Padre Lluc! keep these unknown spells from your heart,—let the forbidden books alone. Instead of the Confessions of Jean Jacques, read the Confessions of St. Augustine,—read the new book, in three volumes, on the Immaculate Conception, which you show me with such ardor, telling me that Can Grande has spoken of it with respect. Beyond the Fathers you must not get, for you have vowed to be a child all your life. Those clear eyes of yours are never to look up into the face of the Eternal Father; the show-box of the Church must content them, with Mary and the saints seen through its dusty glass,—the august figure of the Son, who sometimes reproved his Mother, crowded quite out of sight behind the woman, whom it is so much easier to dress up and exhibit. What is this other book which Parker has read? Padre Doyaguez says, "Hulia, if you read this, you must become a Catholic." Padre Lluc says, "If Parker has read this book, I cannot conceive that he is not a Catholic." The quick Doyaguez then remarks, "Parker is going to Rome to join the Romish Church." Padre Lluc rejoins, "They say so." Hulia Protestante is inclined to cry out, "The day that Parker becomes a Catholic, I too will become one"; but, remembering the rashness of vows and the fallibility of men, she does not adopt that form of expressing *Never.* Parker might, if it pleased God, become a Catholic, and then the world would have two Popes instead of one.

We leave at last the disputed ground of the Library and ascend to the Observatory, which commands a fine view of the city, and a good sweep of the heavens for the telescope, in which Padre Lluc seemed especially to delight. The Observatory is commodious, and is chiefly directed by an attenuated young priest, with a keen eye and hectic cheek; another is occupied in working out mathematical tables;—for these Fathers observe the stars, and are in scientific correspondence with Astronomers in Europe. This circumstance gave us real pleasure on their account,—for science, in all its degrees, is a positive good, and a mental tonic of the first importance. Earnestly did we, in thought, commend it to those wearied minds which have undergone the dialectic dislocations, the denaturalizations of truth and of thought, which enable rational men to become first Catholics, and then Jesuits. For let there be no illusions about strength of mind and so on,—this is effected by means of a vast machinery. As, in the old story, the calves were put in at one end of the cylinder and taken out leather breeches at the other, or as glass is cut and wood carved, so does the raw human material, put into the machine of the Catholic Church, become fashioned according to the will of those who guide it. Hulia Protestante! you have a free step and a clear head; but once go into the machine, and you will come out carved and embossed according to the old traditional pattern,—you as well as another. Where the material is hard, they put on more power,—where it is soft, more care; wherefore I caution you here, as I would in a mill at Lowell or Lawrence,—Don't meddle with the shafts,—don't go too near the wheel,—in short, keep clear of the machinery. And Hulia does so; for, at the last attack of Padre Doyaguez, she suddenly turns upon him and says, "Sir, you are a Doctrinary and a Propagandist." And the good Father suffers her to depart in peace. But first there is the chapel to be seen, with its tawdry and poor ornamentation,—and the dormitories of the scholars, with long double rows of beds and mosquito-nettings. There are two of these, and each of them has at one end a raised platform, with curtains and a bed, where rests and watches the shepherd of the little sheep. Lastly, we have a view of the whole flock, assembled in their play-ground, and one of them, looking up, sees his mother, who has kindly accompanied our visit to the institution. Across the distance that separates us, we see his blue eyes brighten, and, as soon as permission is given, he bounds like a young roe to her arms, shy and tender, his English blood showing through his Spanish skin,—for he is a child of mixed race. We are all pleased and touched, and Padre Lluc presently brings us a daguerreotype, and says, "It is my mother." To us it is an indifferent portrait of an elderly Spanish woman,—but to him, how much! With kindest mutual regard we take leave,—a little surprised, perhaps, to see that Jesuit priests have mothers, and remember them.

CHAPTER VIII.

SAN ANTONIO DE LOS BAÑOS.

"Far from my thoughts, vain world, begone!"

However enchanting Havana may prove when seen through the moonlight of memory, it seems as good a place to go away from as any other, after a stifling night in a net, the wooden shutters left open in the remote hope of air, and admitting the music of a whole opera-troupe of dogs, including Bass, Tenor, Soprano, and Chorus. Instead of bouquets, you throw stones, if you are so fortunate as to have them,—if not, boot-jacks, oranges, your only umbrella. You are last seen thrusting frantic hands and feet through the iron bars, your wife holding you back by the flannel night-gown which you will persist in wearing in this doubtful climate. At last it is over,—the fifth act ends with a howl which makes you hope that some one of the performers has come to grief. But, alas! it is only a stage *dénouement*, whose hero will die again every night while the season lasts. You fall asleep, but the welcome cordial has scarcely been tasted when you are aroused by a knock at the door. It is the night-porter, who wakes you at five by appointment, that you may enjoy your early coffee, tumble into a hired *volante*, and reach, half dead with sleep, the station in time for the train that goes to San Antonio.

Now, whether you are a partisan of early rising or not, you must allow that sunrise and the hour after is the golden time of the day in Cuba. So this hour of starting,—six o'clock,—so distasteful in our latitudes, is a matter of course in tropical climates. Arriving at the station, you encounter new tribulations in the registering and payment of luggage, the transportation of which is not included in the charge for your ticket. Your trunks are recorded in a book, and, having paid a *real* apiece for them, you receive a paper which entitles you to demand them again at your journey's end. The Cuban railways are good, but dear,—the charge being ten cents a mile; whereas in our more favored land one goes for three cents, and has the chance of a collision and surgeon's services without any extra payment. The cars have windows which are always open, and blinds which are always closed, or nearly so. The seats and backs of seats are of cane, for coolness,—hardness being secured at the same time. One reaches San Antonio in an hour and a half, and finds a pleasant village, with a river running through it, several streets of good houses, several more of bad ones, a cathedral, a cockpit, a *volante*, four soldiers on horseback, two on foot, a market, dogs, a bad smell, and lastly, the American Hotel,—a house built in a hollow square, as usual,—kept by a strong-minded woman from the States, whose Yankee thrift is unmistakable, though she has been long absent from the great centres of domestic economy.

Mrs. L——, always on the watch for arrivals, comes out to receive us. We are very welcome, she hints, as far as we go; but why are there not more of us? The smallest favors should be thankfully received, but she hears that Havana is full of strangers, and she wonders, for her part, why people will stay in that hot place, and roast, and stew, and have the yellow fever, when she could make them so comfortable in San Antonio. This want of custom she continues, during our whole visit, to complain of. Would it be uncharitable for us to aver that we found other wants in her establishment which caused us more astonishment, and which went some way towards accounting for the deficiency complained of? wants of breakfast, wants of dinner, wants of something good for tea, wants of towels, wants of candles, wants of ice, or at least of the cooling jars used in the country. Charges exorbitant,—the same as in Havana, where rents are an ounce a week, and upwards; *volantes* difficult,—Mrs. L. having made an agreement with the one livery-stable that they shall always be furnished at most unreasonable prices, of which she, supposably, pockets half. On the other hand, the village is really cool, healthy, and pretty; there are pleasant drives over dreadful roads, if one makes up one's mind to the *volante*, and delightful river-baths, shaded by roofs of palm-tree thatch. One of the best of these is at the foot of Mrs. L.'s inclosure, and its use is included in the privileges of the house. The water is nearly tepid, clear, and green, and the little fish float hither and thither in it,— though men of active minds are sometimes reduced to angle for them, with crooked pins, for amusement. At the hour of one, daily, the ladies of the house betake themselves to this refreshment; and there is laughing, and splashing, and holding of hands, and simulation of all the Venuses that ever were, from the crouching one of the bath, to the triumphant Cytherea, springing for the first time from the wave.

Such are the resources of the house. Those of the neighborhood are various. Foremost among them is the *cafetal*, or coffee-plantation, of Don Juan Torres, distant a league from the village, over which league of stone, sand, and rut you rumble in a *volante* dragged by three horses. You know that the *volante* cannot upset; nevertheless you experience some anxious moments when it leans at an obtuse angle, one wheel in air, one sticking in a hole, the horses balking and kicking, and the postilion swearing his best. But it is written, the *volante* shall not upset,—and so it does not. Long before you see the entrance to the plantation, you watch the tall palms, planted in a line, that shield its borders. An avenue of like growth leads you to the house, where barking dogs announce you, and Don Juan, an elderly gentleman in slippers and a Panama hat, his hair, face, and eyes all faded to one hue of grayness, comes out to accost us. Here, again, Hulia Protestante becomes the subject of a series of attacks, in a new kind. Don Juan first exhausts his flower-garden upon her, and explains all that is new to her. Then she must see his blind Chino, a sightless Samson of a Cooly, who is working resolutely in a mill.

"*Canta!*" says the master, and the poor slave gives tongue like a hound on the scent. "*Baila!*" and, a stick being handed him, he performs the gymnastics of his country, a sort of war-dance without accompaniment. "*El can!*" and, giving him a broom, they loose the dog upon him. A curious tussle then ensues,—the dog attacking furiously, and the blind man, guided by his barking, defending himself lustily. The Chino laughs, the master laughs, but the visitor feels more inclined to cry, having been bred in those Northern habits which respect infirmity. A *real* dismisses the poor soul with a smile, and then begins the journey round the *cafetal*. The coffee-blossom is just in its perfection, and whole acres in sight are white with its flower, which nearly resembles that of the small white jasmine. Its fragrance is said to be delicious after a rain; but, the season being dry, it is scarcely discernible. As shade is a great object in growing coffee, the grounds are laid out in lines of fruit-trees, and these are the ministers of Hulia's tribulation; for Don Juan, whether in kindness or in mischief, insists that she shall taste every unknown fruit,—and as he cuts them and hands them to her, she is forced to obey. First, a little negro shins up a cocoa-nut tree, and flings down the nut, whose water she must drink. One cocoa-nut she endures,—two,—but three? no, she must rebel, and cry out, "*No mi gusta!*" Then she must try a bitter orange, then a sour bitter one, then a sweet lemon, then a huge fruit of triple verjuice flavor. "What is it good for?" she asks, after a shuddering plunge into its acrid depths. "Oh," says the Don, "they eat it in the castors instead of vinegar." Then come *sapotas*, *mamey*, Otaheite gooseberries. "Does she like bananas?" he cuts a tree down with his own hand, and sends the bunch of fruit to her *volante*;—"Sugar-cane?" he bestows a huge bundle of sticks for her leisurely rodentation;—he fills her pocket with coral beans for her children. Having, at last, exhausted every polite attention, and vainly offered gin, rum, and coffee, as a parting demonstration, Hulia and her partner escape, bearing with them many strange flavors, and an agonizing headache, the combined result of sun and acids. Really, if there exist anywhere on earth a Society for the promotion and encouragement of good manners, it should send a diploma to Don Juan, admonishing him only to omit the vinegar-fruit in his further walks of hospitality.

We take the Sunday to visit the nearest Sugar-plantation, belonging to Don Jacinto Gonzales. Sun, not shade, being the desideratum in sugar-planting, there are few trees or shrubs bordering the sugar-fields, which resemble at a distance our own fields of Indian corn, the green of the leaves being lighter, and a pale blue blossom appearing here and there. The points of interest here are the machinery, the negroes, and the work. Entering the sugar-house, we find the *Maquinista* (engineer) superintending some repairs in the machinery, aided by another white man, a Cooly, and an imp of a black boy, who begged of all the party, and revenged himself with clever impertinence on those who refused him. The *Maquinista* was a fine-looking man, from the Pyrenees, very kind and obliging. He told us that Don Jacinto was very old, and came rarely to the plantation. We asked him how the extreme heat of his occupation suited him, and for an answer he opened the bosom of his shirt, and showed us the marks of innumerable leeches. The machinery is not very complicated. It consists of a wheel and band, to throw the canes under the powerful rollers which crush them, and these rollers, three in number, all moved by the steam-engine. The juice flows into large copper caldrons, where it is boiled and skimmed. As they were not at work, we did not see the actual process. Leaving the sugar-house, we went in pursuit of the *Mayoral*, or Overseer, who seemed to inhabit comfortable quarters, in a long, low house, shielded from the sun by a thick screen of matting. We found him a powerful, thick-set man, of surly and uncivil manners, girded with a sword, and further armed with a pistol, a dagger, and a stout whip. He was much too important a person to waste his words upon us, but signified that the major-domo would wait on us, which he presently did. We now entered the Negro quarter, a solid range of low buildings, formed around a hollow square, whose strong entrance is closed at nightfall, and its inmates kept in strict confinement till the morning hour of work comes round. Just within the doorway we encountered the trader, who visits the plantations every Sunday, to tempt the stray cash of the negroes by various commodities, of which the chief seemed to be white bread, calicoes, muslins, and bright cotton handkerchiefs. He told us that their usual weekly expenditure amounted to about twenty-five dollars. Bargaining with him stood the Negro-Driver, a tattooed African, armed with a whip. All within the court swarmed the black bees of the hive,—the men with little clothing, the small children naked, the women decent. All had their little charcoal fires, with pots boiling over them; the rooms within looked dismally dark, close, and dirty; there are no windows, no air and light save through the ever-open door. The beds are sometimes partitioned off by a screen of dried palm-leaf, but I saw no better sleeping-privilege than a board with a blanket or coverlet. From this we turned to the Nursery, where all the children incapable of work are kept. The babies are quite naked, and sometimes very handsome in their way, black and shining, with bright eyes and well-formed limbs. No great provision is made for their amusement, but the little girls nurse them tenderly enough, and now and then the elders fling them a bit of orange or *chaimito*, for which they scramble like so many monkeys. Appeals are constantly made to the pockets of visitors, by open hands stretched out in all directions. To these "*Nada*"—"Nothing"—is the safe reply; for, if you give to one, the others close about you with frantic gesticulation, and you have to break your way through them with some violence, which hurts your own feelings more than it does theirs. On *strict* plantations this is not allowed; but Don Jacinto, like Lord Ashburton at the time of the Maine treaty, is an old man,—a very old man; and where discipline cannot be maintained, peace must be secured on any terms. We visit next the

Sugar-house, where we find the desired condiment in various stages of color and refinement. It is whitened with clay in large funnel-shaped vessels, open at the bottom, to allow the molasses to run off. Above are hogsheads of coarse, dark sugar; below is a huge pit of fermenting molasses, in which rats and small negroes occasionally commit involuntary suicide, and from which rum is made.—N. B. Rum is not a wicked word in Cuba; in Boston everybody is shocked when it is named, and in Cuba nobody is shocked when it is drunk.

And here endeth the description of our visit to the sugar-plantation of Don Jacinto, and in good time, too,—for by this it had grown so hot, that we made a feeble rush for the *volante*, and lay back in it, panting for breath. Encountering a negress with a load of oranges on her head, we bought and ate the fruit with eagerness, though the oranges were bitter. The jolting over three miles of stone and rut did not improve the condition of our aching heads. Arriving at San Antonio, we thankfully went to bed for the rest of the morning, and dreamed, only dreamed, that the saucy black boy in the boiling-house had run after us, had lifted the curtain of the *volante*, screeched a last impertinence after us, and kissed his hand for a good-bye, which, luckily for him, is likely to prove eternal.

CHAPTER IX.

THE MORRO FORTRESS—THE UNIVERSITY OF HAVANA—THE BENEFICENZA.

THE Spanish government experiences an unwillingness to admit foreigners into the Morro, their great stronghold, the causes of which may not be altogether mysterious. Americans have been of late especially excluded from it, and it was only by a fortunate chance that we were allowed to visit it. A friend of a friend of ours happened to have a friend in the garrison, and, after some delays and negotiations, an early morning hour was fixed upon for the expedition.

The Fort is finely placed at the entrance of the harbor, and is in itself a picturesque object. It is built of a light, yellowish stone, which is seen, as you draw near, in strong contrast with the vivid green of the tropical waters. We approached it by water, taking a row-boat from the Alameda. As we passed, we had a good view of a daily Havana spectacle, the washing of the horses. This being by far the easiest and most expeditious way of cleaning the animals, they are driven daily to the sea in great numbers, those of one party being tied together; they disport themselves in the surge and their wet backs glisten in the sun. Their drivers, nearly naked, plunge in with them, and bring them safely back to the shore.

But for the Morro. We entered without difficulty, and began at once a somewhat steep ascent, which the heat, even at that early hour, made laborious. After some climbing, we reached the top of the parapet, and looked out from the back of the Fortress. On this side, if ever on any, it will be taken,—for, standing with one's back to the harbor, one sees, nearly on the right hand, a point where trenches could be opened with advantage. The Fort is heavily gunned and garrisoned, and seems to be in fighting order. The outer wall is separated from the inner by a paved space some forty feet in width. The height of both walls makes this point a formidable one; but scaling-ladders could be thrown across, if one had possession of the outer wall. The material is the coralline rock common in this part of the island. It is a soft stone, and would prove, it is feared, something like the cotton-bag defence of New Orleans memory,—as the balls thrown from without would sink in, and not splinter the stone, which for the murderous work were to be wished. A little perseverance, with much perspiration, brought us to a high point called the Lantern, which is merely a small room, where the telescope, signal-books, and signals are kept. Here we were received by an official in blue spectacles and with a hole in his boot, but still with that air of being the chiefest thing on God's earth common to all Spaniards. The best of all was that we had brought a sack of oranges with us, and that the time was now come for their employment. With no other artillery than these did we take the very heart of the Morro citadel,—for on offering them to the official with the hole, he surrendered at once, smiled, gave us seats, and sitting down with us, indeed, was soon in the midst of his half-dozenth orange. Having refreshed ourselves, examined the flags of all nations, and made all the remarks which our limited Spanish allowed, we took leave, redescended, and reëmbarked. One of our party, an old soldier, had meanwhile been busily scanning the points and angles of the fortress, pacing off distances, etc., etc. The result of his observations would, no doubt, be valuable to men of military minds. But the writer of this, to be candid, was especially engaged with the heat, the prospect, the oranges, and the soldiers' wives and children, who peeped out from windows here and there. Such trifling creatures do come into such massive surroundings, and trifle still!

Our ladies, being still in a furious mood of sight-seeing, desired to visit the University of Havana, and, having made appointment with an accomplished Cuban, betook themselves to the College buildings with all proper escort. Their arrival in the peristyle occasioned some excitement. One of the students came up, and said in good English, "What do you want?" Others, not so polite, stared and whispered in corners. A message to one of the professors was attended with some delay, and our Cuban friend, having gone to consult with him, returned to say, with some embarrassment, that the professor would be happy to show the establishment to the ladies on Sunday, at two P. M., when every male creature but himself would be out of it; but as for their going through the rooms while the undergraduates were about, that was not to be thought of. "Why not?" asked the ladies. "For your own sake," said the messenger, and proceeded to explain that the appearance of the *skirted* in these halls of learning would be followed by such ill-conduct and indignity of impertinence on the part of the *shirted* as might be intolerable to the one and disadvantageous to the other. Now there be women, we know, whose horrid fronts could have awed these saucy little Cubans into decency and good behavior, and some that we wot of, whether possessing that power or not, would have delighted in the fancied exercise of it. What strong-minded company, under these circumstances, would have turned back? What bolting, tramping, and rushing would they not have made through the ranks of the astonished professors and students? The Anniversary set, for example, who sweep the pews of men, or, coming upon one forlorn, crush him as a boa does a sheep. Our silly little flock only laughed, colored, and retreated to the *volantes*, where they held a council of war, and decided to go visit some establishment where possibly better manners might prevail.

Returning on the Sunday at the hour appointed, they walked through the deserted building, and found spacious rooms, the pulpits of the professors, the benches of the students, the Queen's portrait, a very limited library, and for all consolation, some pleasant Latin sentences over the doors of the various departments, celebrating the solace and delights of learning. This was seeing the College, literally; but it was a good deal like seeing the Lion's den, the Lion himself being absent on leave,—or like visiting the Hippopotamus in Regent's Park on those days in which he remains steadfastly buried in his tank, and will show only the tip of a nostril for your entrance-fee. Still, it was a pleasure to know that learning was so handsomely housed; and as for the little rabble who could not be trusted in the presence of the sex, we forgave them heartily, knowing that soberer manners would one day come upon them as inevitably as baldness and paternity.

Let me here say that a few days in Havana make clear to one the seclusion of women in the East, and its causes. Wherever the animal vigor of men is so large in proportion to their moral power as in those countries, women must be glad to forego their liberties for the protection of the strong arm. One master is better for them than many. Whatever tyranny may grow out of such barbarous manners, the institution springs from a veritable necessity and an original good intention. The Christian religion should change this, which is justifiable only in a Mohammedan country. But where that religion is so loosely administered as in Cuba, where its teachers themselves frequent the cockpit and the gaming-table, one must not look for too much of its power in the manners and morals of men.

The Beneficenza was our next station. It is, as its name signifies, an institution with a benevolent purpose, an orphan asylum and foundling hospital in one. The State here charitably considers that infants who are abandoned by their parents are as much orphaned as they can become by the interposition of death,—nay, more. The death of parents oftenest leaves a child with some friend or relative; but the foundling is cut off from all human relationship,— he belongs only to the hand that takes him up, where he has been left to die. Despite the kind cruelty of modern theories, which will not allow of suitable provision for the sufferer, for fear of increasing the frequency of the crime by which he suffers, our hearts revolt at the miserable condition of these little creatures in our great cities, confounded with hopeless pauperism in its desolate asylums, or farmed out to starve and die. They belong to the State, and the State should nobly retrieve the world's offence against them. Their broken galaxy shows many a bright star here and there. Such a little wailing creature has been found who has commanded great actions and done good service among men. Let us then cherish the race of foundlings, of whom Moses was the first and the greatest. The princess who reared him saw not the glorious destiny which lay hid, as a birth-jewel, in his little basket of reeds. She saw only, as some of us have seen, a helpless, friendless babe. When he dedicated to her his first edition of the Pentateuch—— But nay, he did not; for neither gratitude nor dedications were in fashion among the Jews.

We found the Beneficenza spacious, well-ventilated, and administered with great order. It stands near the sea, with a fine prospect in view, and must command a cool breeze, if there be any. The children enjoy sea-bathing in summer. The Superintendent received us most kindly, and presented us to the Sisters who have charge of the children, who were good specimens of their class. We walked with them through the neat dormitories, and observed that they were much more airy than those of the Jesuit College, lately described. They all slept on the sackings of cots, beds being provided only in the infirmary. In the latter place we found but two inmates,—one suffering from ordinary Cuban fever, the other from ophthalmia.—N. B. Disease of the eyes does not seem to be common in Cuba, in spite of the tropical glare of the sun; nor do people nurse and complain of their eyes there, as with us. We found a separate small kitchen for the sick, which was neat and convenient. The larger kitchen too was handsomely endowed with apparatus, and the Superintendent told us, with a twinkle in his eye, that the children lived well. Coffee at six, a good breakfast at nine, dinner at the usual hour, bread and coffee before bed-time;—this seemed very suitable as to quantity, though differing from our ideas of children's food; but it must be remembered that the nervous stimulus of coffee is not found to be excessive in hot climates; it seems to be only what Nature demands,—no more. The kind Nun who accompanied us now showed us, with some pride, various large presses set in the wall, and piled to the top with clean and comfortable children's clothing. We came presently to where the boys were reciting their catechism. An Ecclesiastic was hearing them;—they seemed ready enough with their answers, but were allowed to gabble off the holy words in a manner almost unintelligible, and quite indecorous. They were bright, healthy-looking little fellows, ranging apparently from eight to twelve years of age. They had good play-ground set off for them, and shady galleries to walk up and down in. Coming from their quarter, the girls' department seemed quiet enough. Here was going on the eternal task of needle-work, to which the sex has been condemned ever since Adam's discovery of his want of wardrobe. Oh, ye wretched, foolish women! why will ye forever sew? "We must not only sew, but be thankful to sew; *that little needle* being, as the sentimental Curtis has said, the only thing between us and the worst that may befall."

These incipient women were engaged in various forms of sewing,—the most skilful in a sort of embroidery, like that which forms the border of *piña* handkerchiefs. A few were reading and spelling. One poor blind girl sat amongst them, with melancholy arms folded, and learned nothing,—they told us, nothing; for the instruction of the blind is not thought of in these parts. This seemed piteous to us, and made us reflect how happy are *our*

Blinds, to say nothing of our Deafs and Dumbs. Idiocy is not uncommon here, and is the result of continual intermarriage between near relations; but it will be long before they will provide it with a separate asylum and suitable instruction.

But now came the saddest part of the whole exhibition,—a sight common enough in Europe, but by some accident hitherto unseen by us. Here is a sort of receptacle, with three or four compartments, which turns on a pivot. One side of it is open to the street, and in it the wretched parent lays the more wretched baby,—ringing a small bell at the same time, for the new admittance. The parent vanishes, the receptacle turns on its pivot,—the baby is within, and, we are willing to believe, in merciful hands.

The sight of this made, for the first time, the crime real to me. I saw at a flash the whole tragedy of desertion,—the cautious approach, the frightened countenance, the furtive act, and the great avenging pang of Nature after its consummation. What was Hester Prynne's pillory, compared to the heart of any of these mothers? I thought too of Rousseau, bringing to such a place as this children who had the right to inherit divine genius, and deserting them for the sordid reason that he did not choose to earn their bread;—the helpless mother weeping at home, and begging, through long years, to be allowed to seek and reclaim them.

Well, here were the little creatures kindly cared for; yet what a piteous place was their nursery! Some of the recent arrivals looked as if ill-usage had been exhausted upon them before they were brought hither. Blows and drugs and starvation had been tried upon them, but, with the tenacity of infancy, they clung to life. They would not die;—well then, they should live to regret it. Some of them lay on the floor, deformed and helpless; the older ones formed a little class, and were going through some elementary exercise when we passed. The babies had a large room allotted to them, and I found the wet-nurses apportioned one to each child. This appeared a very generous provision, as in such establishments elsewhere, three and even four children are given to one nurse. They had comfortable cribs, on each of which was pinned the name of its little inmate, and the date of its entrance;—generally, the name and age of the child are found written on a slip of paper attached to its clothing, when it is left in the receptacle. I saw on one, "Cecilio, three weeks old." He had been but a few days in the establishment.

Of course, I lingered longest in the babies' room, and longest of all near the crib of the little Cecilio. He was a pretty baby, and seemed to me the most ill-used of all, because the youngest. "Could they not bear with you three weeks, little fellow?" I said. "I know those at whose firesides such as you would have been welcome guests. That New York woman whom I met lately, young, rich, and childless,—I could commend you to her in place of the snarling little spaniel fiend who was her constant care and companion."

But here the Superintendent made a polite bow, saying,—"And now your Worships have seen all; for the chapel is undergoing repairs, and cannot be visited." And so we thanked, and departed.

CHAPTER X.

CAN GRANDE'S DEPARTURE.—THE DOMINICA.—LOTTERY-TICKETS.

I HAVE not told you how Can Grande took leave of the Isle of Rogues, as one of our party christened the fair Queen of the Antilles. I could not tell you how he loathed the goings on at Havana, how hateful he found the Spaniards, and how villanous the American hotel-keepers. His superlatives of censure were in such constant employment that they began to have a threadbare sound before he left us; and as he has it in prospective to run the gauntlet of all the innkeepers on the continent of Europe, to say nothing of further lands, where innkeepers would be a relief, there is no knowing what exhaustion his powers in this sort may undergo before he reaches us again. He may break down into weak, compliant good-nature, and never be able to abuse anybody again, as long as he lives. In that case, his past life and his future, taken together, will make a very respectable average. But the climate really did not suit him, the company did not satisfy, and there came a moment when he said, "I can bear it no longer!" and we answered, "Go in peace!"

It now becomes me to speak of Sobrina, who has long been on a temperance footing, and who forgets even to blush when the former toddy is mentioned, though she still shudders at the remembrance of sour-sop. She is the business-man of the party; and while philosophy and highest considerations occupy the others, with an occasional squabble over virtue and the rights of man, she changes lodgings, hires carts, transports luggage, and, knowing half-a-dozen words of Spanish, makes herself clearly comprehensible to everybody. "We have found a Spanish steamer for Can Grande;" but she rows thither in a boat and secures his passage and state-room. The noontide sun is hot upon the waters, but her zeal is hotter still. Now she has made a curious bargain with her boatmen, by which they are to convey the whole party to the steamer on the fourth day.

"What did you tell them?" we asked.

"I said, *tres noches* (three nights) and *un dia*, (one day,) and then took out my watch and showed them five o'clock on it, and pointed to the boat and to myself. They understood perfectly."

And so, in truth, they did; for, going to the wharf on the day and at the hour appointed, we found the boatmen in waiting, with eager faces. But here a new difficulty presented itself;—the runner of our hotel, a German whose Cuban life has sharpened his wits and blunted his conscience, insisted that the hiring of boats for the lodgers was one of his (many) perquisites, and that before his sovereign prerogative all other agreements were null and void.—N. B. There was always something experimentative about this man's wickedness. He felt that he did not know how far men might be gulled, or the point where they would be likely to resist. This was a fault of youth. With increasing years and experience he will grow bolder and more skilful, and bids fair, we should say, to become one of the most dexterous operators known in his peculiar line. On the present occasion he did not heed the piteous pleadings of the disappointed boatmen, nor Sobrina's explanations, nor Can Grande's arguments. But when the whole five of us fixed upon him our mild and scornful eyes, something within him gave way. He felt a little bit of the moral pressure of Boston, and feebly broke down, saying, "You better do as you like, then," and so the point was carried.

A pleasant row brought us to the side of the steamer. It was dusk already as we ascended her steep gangway, and from that to darkness there is, at this season, but the interval of a breath. Dusk too were our thoughts, at parting from Can Grande, the mighty, the vehement, the great fighter. How were we to miss his deep music, here and at home! With his assistance we had made a very respectable band; now we were to be only a wandering drum and fife,—the fife particularly shrill, and the drum particularly solemn. Well, we went below, and examined the little den where Can Grande was to pass the other seven days of his tropical voyaging. The berths were arranged the wrong way,—across, not along, the vessel,—and we foresaw that his head would go up and his feet down, and *vice versâ*, with every movement of the steamer, and our weak brains reeled at the bare thought of what he was to suffer. He, good soul, meanwhile was thinking of his supper, and wondering if he could get tea, coffee, and chocolate, a toasted roll, and the touch of cold ham which an invalid loves. And we beheld, and they were bringing up the side of the vessel trays of delicious pastry, and festoons of fowls, with more literal butcher's meat. And we said, "There will be no famine on board. Make the most of your supper, Can Grande; for it will be the last of earth to you, for some time to come." And now came silence, and tears, and last embraces; we slipped down the gangway into our little craft, and looking up, saw bending above us, between the slouched hat and the silver beard, the eyes that we can never forget, that seemed to drop back in the darkness with the solemnity of a last farewell. We went home, and the drum hung himself gloomily on his peg, and the little fife *shut up* for the remainder of the evening.

Has Mr. Dana described the Dominica, I wonder? Well, if he has, I cannot help it. He never can have eaten so many ices there as I have, nor passed so many patient hours amid the screeching, chattering, and devouring, which make it most like a cage of strange birds, or the monkey department in the Jardin des Plantes.—*Mem.* I always observed that the monkeys just mentioned seemed far more mirthful than their brethren in the London

Zoological Gardens. They form themselves, so to speak, on a livelier model, and feel themselves more at home with their hosts.

But the Dominica. You know, probably, that it is the great *café* of Havana. All the day long it is full of people of all nations, sipping ices, chocolate, and so on; and all night long, also, up to the to me very questionable hour when its patrons go home and its *garçons* go to bed. We often found it a welcome refuge at noon, when the *douche* of sunlight on one's *cervix* bewilders the faculties, and confuses one's principles of gravitation, toleration, etc., etc. You enter from the Tophet of the street, and the intolerable glare is at once softened to a sort of golden shadow. The floor is of stone; in the midst trickles a tiny fountain with gilded network; all other available space is crowded with marble tables, square or round; and they in turn are scarcely visible for the swarm of black-coats that gather round them. The smoke of innumerable cigars gives a Rembrandtic tinge to the depths of the picture, and the rows and groups of nodding Panama hats are like very dull flower-beds. In the company, of course, the Spanish-Cuban element largely predominates; yet here and there the sharper English breaks upon the ear.

"Yes, I went to that plantation; but they have only one thousand boxes of sugar, and we want three thousand for our operation."

A Yankee, you say. Yes, certainly; and turning, you see the tall, strong Philadelphian from our hotel, who calls for everything by its right name, and always says, "*Mas! mas!*" when the waiter helps him to ice. Some one near us is speaking a fuller English, with a richer "*r*" and deeper intonation. See there! that is our own jolly captain, Brownless of ours, the King of the "Karnak"; and going up to the British lion, we shake the noble beast heartily by the paw.

The people about us are imbibing a variety of cooling liquids. Our turn comes at last. The *garçon* who says, "I speke Aingliss," brings us each a delicious orange *granizada*, a sort of half-frozen water-ice, familiar to Italy, but unknown in America. It is ice in the first enthusiasm of freezing,—condensed, not hardened. Promoting its liquefaction with the spoon, you enjoy it through the mediation of a straw. The unskilful make strange noises and gurglings through this *tenuis avena*; but to those who have not forgotten the accomplishment of suction, as acquired at an early period of existence, the *modus in quo* is easy and agreeable.

You will hardly weary of watching the groups that come and go, and sit and talk in this dreamy place. If you are a lady, every black eye directs its full, tiresome stare at your face, no matter how plain that face may be. But you have learned before this to consider those eyes as so many black dots, so many marks of wonder with no sentence attached; and so you coolly pursue your philosophizing in your corner, strong in the support of a companion who, though deeply humanitarian and peaceful, would not hesitate to punch any number of Spanish heads that should be necessary for the maintenance of your comfort and his dignity.

The scene is occasionally varied by the appearance of a beggar-woman, got up in great decency, and with a wonderful air of pinched and faded gentility. She wears an old shawl upon her head, but it is as nicely folded as an aristocratic mantilla; her feet are cased in the linen slippers worn by the poorer classes, but there are no unsavory rags and dirt about her. "That good walk of yours, friend," I thought, "does not look like starvation." Yet, if ever there were a moment when one's heart should soften towards an imposing fellow-creature, it is when one is in the midst of the orange *granizada*. The beggar circles slowly and mournfully round all the marble tables in turn, holding out her hand to each, as the plate is offered at a church collection. She is not importunate; but looking in each one's face, seems to divine whether he will give or no. A Yankee, sitting with a Spaniard, offers her his cigar. The Spaniard gravely pushes the cigar away, and gives her a *medio*.

More pertinacious is the seller of lottery-tickets, male or female, who has more at stake, and must run the risk of your displeasure for the chance of your custom. Even in your bed you are hardly safe from the ticket-vender. You stand at your window, and he, waiting in the street, perceives you, and with nods, winks, and showing of his wares endeavors to establish a communication with you. Or you stop and wait somewhere in your *volante*, and in the twinkling of an eye the wretch is at your side, to bear you company till you drive off again. At the Dominica he is especially persevering, and stands and waits with as much zeal as if he knew the saintly line of Milton. Like the beggar, however, he is discriminative in the choice of his victims, and persecutes the stony Yankee less than the oily Spaniard, whose inbred superstitions force him to believe in luck.

Very strange stories do they tell about the trade in lottery-tickets,—strange at least to us, who consider them the folly of follies. Here, as in Italy, the lotteries are under the care of the State, and their administration is as careful and important as that of any other branch of finance. They are a regular and even reputable mode of investment. The wealthy commercial houses all own tickets, sometimes keeping the same number for years, but more frequently changing after each unsuccessful experiment. A French gentleman in Havana assured me that his tickets had already cost him seven thousand dollars. "And now," said he, "I cannot withdraw, for I cannot lose what I have already paid. The number has not been up once in eight years; its turn must come soon. If I were to sell my ticket, some one would be sure to draw the great prize with it the week after." This, perhaps, is not very unlike the calculations of business risks most in vogue in our great cities. A single ticket costs an ounce (seventeen dollars); but you are constantly offered fractions, to an eighth or a sixteenth. There are ticket-brokers who accommodate the poorer classes with interests to the amount of ten cents, and so on. Thus, for them, the lottery replaces the savings-bank, with entire uncertainty of any return, and the demoralizing process of expectation thrown into the bargain. The negroes invest a good deal of money in this way, and we heard in Matanzas a curious anecdote on this head. A number of negroes, putting their means together, had commissioned a ticket-broker to purchase and hold for them a certain ticket. After long waiting and paying up, news came to Matanzas that the ticket had drawn the $100,000 prize. The owners of the negroes were in despair at this intelligence. "Now my cook will buy himself," says one; "my *calesero* will be free," says another; and so on. The poor slaves ran, of course, in great agitation, to get their money. But, lo! the office was shut up. The rascal broker had absconded. He had never run the risk of purchasing the ticket; but had coolly appropriated this and similar investments to his own use, preferring the bird in the hand to the whole aviary of possibilities. He was never heard of more; but should he ever turn up anywhere, I commend him as the fittest subject for Lynch-law on record.

Well, as I have told you, all these golden chances wait for you at the Dominica, and many Americans buy, and look very foolish when they acknowledge it. The Nassauese all bought largely during their short stay; and even their little children held up with exultation their fragments of tickets, all good for something, and bad for something, too.

If you visit the Dominica in the evening, you find the same crowd, only with a sprinkling of women, oftenest of your own country, in audacious bonnets, and with voices and laughter which bring the black eyes upon them for a time. If it be Sunday evening, you will see here and there groups of ladies in full ball-dress, fresh from the Paseo, the *volante* waiting for them outside. All is then at its gayest and busiest; but your favorite waiter, with disappointment in his eyes, will tell you that there is "*no mas*" of your favorite *granizada*, and will persuade you to take I know not what nauseous substitute in its place; for all ices are not good at the Dominica, and some are (excuse the word) nasty. People sit and sip, prolonging their pleasures with dilatory spoon and indefatigable tongue. Group follows group; but the Spaniards are what I should call heavy sitters, and tarry long over their ice or chocolate. The waiter invariably brings to every table a chafing-dish with a burning coal, which will light a cigar long after its outer glow has subsided into ashy white. Some humans retain this kindling power;—*vide* Ninon and the ancient Goethe;—it is the heart of fire, not the flame of beauty, that does it. When one goes home, tired, at ten or eleven, the company shows no sign of thinning, nor does one imagine how the ground is ever cleared, so as to allow an interval of sleep between the last ice at night and the first coffee in the morning. It is the universal *siesta* which makes the Cubans so bright and fresh in the evening. With all this, their habits are sober, and the evening refreshment always light.

No suppers are eaten here; and it is even held dangerous to take fruit as late as eight o'clock, P. M.

The Dominica has still another aspect to you, when you go there in the character of a Citizen and Head of family to order West India sweetmeats for home-consumption. You utter the magic word *dulces*, and are shown with respect into the establishment across the way, where a neat steam-engine is in full operation, tended by blacks and whites, stripped above the waist, and with no superfluous clothing below it. Here they grind the chocolate, and make the famous preserves, of which a list is shown you, with prices affixed. As you will probably lose some minutes in perplexity as to which are best for you to order, let me tell you that the guava jelly and marmalade are first among them, and there is no second. You may throw in a little pine-apple, mamey, lime, and cocoa-plum; but the guava is the thing, and, in case of a long run on the tea-table, will give the most effectual support. The limes used to be famous in our youth; but in these days they make them hard and tough. The marmalade of bitter oranges is one of the most useful of Southern preserves; but I do not remember it on the list of the Dominica. Having given your order, let me further advise you to remain, if practicable, and see it fulfilled; as you will otherwise find divers trifling discrepancies between the bill and the goods delivered, which, though of course purely accidental, will all be, somehow, to the Dominica's advantage, and not to yours. If you are in moderate circumstances, order eight or ten dollars' worth; if affluent, twenty or thirty dollars' worth; if rash and extravagant, you may rise even to sixty dollars; but you will find in such an outlay food for repentance. One word in your ear: do not buy the syrups, for they are made with very bad sugar, and have no savor of the fruits they represent.

And this is all I can tell about the Dominica, which I recommend to all of you for refreshment and amusement. We have nothing like it in New York or Boston,—our *salons* of the same description having in them much more to eat, and much less to see. As I look back upon it, the place assumes a deeply Moorish aspect. I see the fountain, the golden light, the dark faces, and intense black eyes, a little softened by the comforting distance. Oh! to sit there for one hour, and help the *garçon's* bad English, and be pestered by the beggar, and tormented by the ticket-vender, and support the battery of the wondering looks, which make it sin for you, a woman, to be abroad by day! Is there any Purgatory which does not grow lovely as you remember it? Would not a man be hanged twice, if he could?

CHAPTER XI.

COMPANY AT THE HOTEL.—SERVANTS.— OUR DRIVE.—DON PEPE.

I DO not mean to give portraits of the individuals at our hotel. My chance acquaintance with them confers on me no right to appropriate their several characteristics for my own convenience and the diversion of the public. I will give only such general sketches as one may make of a public body at a respectful distance, marking no features that can fix or offend.

Our company is almost entirely composed of two classes,—invalids and men of business, with or without their families. The former are easily recognizable by their sad eyes and pallid countenances; even the hectic of disease does not deceive you,—it has no affinity to the rose of health. There is the cough, too,—the cruel cough that would not be left at the North, that breaks out through all the smothering by day, and shakes the weak frame with uneasy rocking by night.

The men of business are apt to name their firm, when they introduce themselves to you.

"My name is Norval, Sir,—Norval, Grampian, & Company. I suppose you know the firm."

"We do not, indeed; but we murmur, in return, that we have an Uncle or a Cousin in business, who may, very likely, know it.

"What is your Uncle's firm?" will be the next question.

"Philpots Brothers."

"Excellent people,—we have often done business with them. Happy to make your acquaintance, Sir."

And so, the first preliminaries being established, and each party assured of the other's solvency, we glide easily into a relation of chat and kind little mutualities which causes the periods of contact to pass smoothly enough.

We found among these some manly, straightforward fellows, to whom one would confide one's fortunes, or even one's widow and orphans, with small fear of any flaw in their trustworthiness. Nor was the more slippery class, we judged, without its representatives; but of this we had only hints, not experience. There were various day-boarders, who frequented our table only, and lodged elsewhere. A few of these were decorous Spaniards, who did not stare, nor talk, nor gobble their meals with unbecoming vivacity of appetite. They were obviously staid business-men, differing widely in character from the street Spaniard, whom I have already copiously described. Some were Germans, thinned by the climate, and sharpened up to the true Yankee point of competition; very little smack of Father-land was left about them,—no song, no sentimentality, not much quivering of the heart-strings at remembrance of the old folks at home, whom some of them have not seen in twenty years, and will never see again. To be sure, in such a hard life as theirs, with no social surroundings, and grim Death meeting them at every corner, there is nothing for it but to be as hard and tough as one's circumstances. But give me rather the German heart in the little old German village, with the small earnings and spendings, the narrow sphere of life and experience, and the great vintage of geniality which is laid up from youth to age, and handed down with the old wine from father to son. I don't like your cosmopolitan German any better than I do your Englishman done to death with travel. I prize the home-flavor in all the races that are capable of home. There are very many Germans scattered throughout Cuba, in various departments of business. They are generally successful, and make very good Yankees, in the technical acceptation of the word. Their original soundness of constitution enables them to resist the climate better than Americans, and though they lose flesh and color, they rarely give that evidence of a disordered liver which foreign residents in tropical countries are so apt to show.

The ladies at the hotel were all our own countrywomen, as we see them at home and abroad. I have already spoken of their diligence in sewing, and of their enthusiasm in shopping. Their other distinctive features are too familiar to us to require illustration. Yet upon one trait I will adventure. A group of them sat peaceably together, one day, when a file of newspapers arrived, with full details of a horrible Washington scandal, and the murder consequent upon it. Now I must say that no swarm of bees ever settled upon a bed of roses more eagerly than our fair sisters pounced upon the carrion of that foul and dreadful tale. It flew from hand to hand and from mouth to mouth, as if it had been glad tidings of great joy,—and the universal judgment upon it caused our heart to shudder with the remembrance that we had heard some one somewhere propose that female offenders should be tried by a jury of their own sex.

It was a real comfort, a few days later, to hear this sad subject discussed by a circle of intelligent Englishwomen, with good sense and good feeling, and with true appreciation of the twofold crime, the domestic treason and the public assassination. In passing, I must say of this English circle that it is charming, and that the Britannic Consul has the key of it in his pocket. Wherefore, if any of you, my friends, would desire to know four of the most charming women in Havana, he is to lay hold upon Mr. Consul Crawford, and compel him to become his friend.

Mr. Dana recounts his shopping in Havana, whereof the beginning and ending were one dress, white and blue, which he commendably purchased for his wife. But does Dana know what he had to be thankful for, in getting off with one dress? Tell him, ye patient husbands, whose pockets seem to be made like lemons, only to be squeezed! Tell him, ye insatiate ones, who have new wants and new ideas every day! Dana's dress was, probably, an *holan batista*, which he calls "*Bolan*";—it was, in other words, a figured linen cambric. But you have bought those cambrics by the piece, and also *piñas*, thin, gossamer fabrics, of all degrees of color and beauty, sometimes with *pattern flounces*,—do you hear? And you have bought Spanish table-cloths with red or blue edges, with bull-fights on them, and balloon-ascensions, and platoons of soldiery in review, and with bull-fighting and ballooning napkins to match. And you have secured such bales of transparent white muslins, that one would think you intended to furnish a whole troupe of ballet-girls with saucer petticoats. Catalan lace you have got, to trim curtains, sheets, pillow-cases, and kitchen-towels with. And as for your fans, we only hope that the stories you tell about them are true, and that Kitty, Julia, and Jemima at home are to divide them with you; for we shrewdly suspect that you mean, after all, to keep them, and to have a fan for every day in the year. Let a man reflect upon all this, added to the inevitable three dollars and fifty cents *per diem*, with the frequent refreshment of *volantes* and ices at the Dominica, and then say whether it pays to take a partner, not of a frugal mind, to Havana for the season.

I had intended to give some account of the servants at Mrs. Almy's; but my gossip runs to such lengths that I must dismiss them with a few words. Ramon, the porter, never leaves the vestibule; he watches there all day, takes his meals there, plays cards there in the evening with his fellow-servants, and at night spreads his cot there, and lies down to sleep. He is white, as are most of the others. If I have occasion to go into the kitchen at night, I find a cot there also, with no bed, and a twisted sheet upon it, which, I am told, is the chrysalis of the cook. Said cook is a free yellow, from Nassau, who has wrought in this kitchen for many years past. Heat, hard work, and they say drink, have altogether brought him to a bad pass. His legs are frightfully swollen, and in a few days he leaves, unable to continue his function. Somebody asks after his wife. "She has got a white husband now," he tells us, with a dejected air. She might have waited a little,—he is to die soon.

Garcia is the kind waiter with the rather expressive face, who is never weary of bringing us the rice and fried plantain which form, after all, the staple of our existence in Cuba. The waiters all do as well as they can, considering the length of the table, and the extremely short staple of the boarders' patience. As a general rule, they understand good English better than bad Spanish; but comparative philology has obviously been neglected among them.

Luis is a negro boy of twelve, fearfully black in the face and white in the eye; his wool cropped to entire bareness. He is chiefly good at dodging your orders,—disappears when anything is asked for, but does not return with it.

Rosalia is the chambermaid, of whom I have already spoken, as dexterous in sweeping the mosquitos from the nets,—her afternoon service. She brings, too, the morning cup of coffee, and always says, "Good morning, Sir; you want coffee?"—the only English she can speak. Her voice and smile are particularly sweet, her person tall and well-formed, and her face comely and modest. She is not altogether black,—about mahogany color. I mention her modesty because, so far as I saw, the good-looking ones among the black women have an air of assumption, and almost of impudence,—probably the result of flattery.

With all this array of very respectable "help," our hostess avers that she has not a single person about her whom she can trust. Hence the weary look about her eyes and brow, speaking of a load never laid down. She attends to every detail of business herself, and is at work over her books long after her boarders have retired to rest.

But the one of all the servants who interests us most is Alexander, Mrs. Almy's own slave. He is, like Rosalia, of mahogany color, with a broad forehead and intelligent eyes. His proud, impatient nature is little suited to his position, and every day brings some new account of his petulant outbreaks. To-day he quarrelled with the new cook, and drew a knife upon him. Mrs. Almy threatens continually to sell him, and at this the hearts of some of us grow very sick,—for she always says that his spirit must be broken, that only the severest punishment will break it, and that she cannot endure to send him to receive that punishment. What that mysterious ordeal may be, we dare not question,—we who cannot help him from it; we can only wish that he might draw that knife across his own throat before he undergoes it. He is trying to buy his own freedom, and has something saved towards it. He looks as if he would do good service, with sufficient training. As it is, he probably knows no law, save the two conflicting ones, of necessity and his own wild passions. One of the sad thoughts we shall carry away from here will be that Alexander is to be sold, and his spirit broken. Good Mrs. Almy, do have a little patience with him! Enlighten his dark mind; let Christianity be taught him, which will show him, even in his slave's estate, that he can conquer his fellow-servant better than by drawing a knife upon him. Set him free? Ah! that is past praying for; but, as he has the right to buy himself, give him every chance of doing so, and we, your petitioners, will pray for him, and for you who need it, with that heavy brow of care.

I have called the negroes of Nassau ugly, clumsy, and unserviceable. The Cuban negroes make, so far, a very different impression upon me. One sees among them considerable beauty of form, and their faces are more expressive and better cut than those of the Nassau blacks. The women are well-made, and particularly well-poised, standing perfectly straight from top to toe, with no hitch or swing in their gait. Beauty of feature is not so common among them; still, one meets with it here and there. There is a massive sweep in the bust and arms of the women which is very striking. Even in their faces, there is a certain weight of feature and of darkness, which makes its own impression. The men have less grace of movement, though powerful and athletic in their make. Those who are employed at hard work, within-doors, wear very little clothing, being stripped to the loins. One often has a glimpse of them, in passing the open smithies and wheelwrights' shops. The greatest defect among the men is the want of calf. The narrow boots of the postilions make this particularly discernible. Such a set of spindleshanks I never saw, not even in Trumbull's famous Declaration of Independence, in which we have the satisfaction of assuring ourselves that the fathers of our liberty had two legs apiece, and crossed them in concert with the utmost regularity. One might think, at first, that these narrow boots were as uncomfortable to the *calesero* as the Scottish instrument of torture of that name; but his little swagger when he is down, and his freedom in kicking when he is up, show that he has ample room in them.

Very jolly groups of Spanish artisans does one see in the open shops at noon, gathered around a table. The board is chiefly adorned with earthen jars of an ancient pattern filled with oil and wine, platters of bread and sausage,—and the ever fragrant onion is generally perceptible. The personal qualities of these men are quite unknown to us; but they have an air of good-fellowship which gives pleasure.

We hired a carriage this afternoon,—we and two others from Boston. We had a four-wheeled barouche, with two horses, which costs two dollars an hour; whereas a *volante* can be hired only at eight dollars and a half per whole afternoon,—no less time, no less money. As it holds but two, or, at the utmost, three, this is paying rather dear for the glory of showing one's self on the Paseo. The moment we were in the carriage, our coachman nodded to us, and saying, "*A la tropa*," galloped off with us in an unknown direction. We soon fell in with a line of other carriages, and concluded that there was something to be seen somewhere, and that we were going to see it. Nor were we mistaken; for in due time, ascending a steep acclivity, we came upon "*la tropa*," and found some ten thousand soldiers undergoing review, in their seersucker coats and Panama hats, which, being very like the costume of an easy Wall-Street man in August, had a very peaceful appearance on so military an occasion. The cavalry and infantry had nearly concluded their evolutions when we arrived. The troops were spread out on a vast plateau. The view was magnificent. The coachman pointed to one immovable figure on horseback, and said, "Concha." We found it was indeed the Captain-General; for as the different bands passed, they all saluted him, and he returned their courtesy. Unluckily, his back was towards us, and so remained until he rode off in an opposite direction. He was mounted on a white horse, and was dressed like the others. He seemed erect and well-made; but his back, after all, was very like any one else's back. *Query*,—Did we see Concha, or did we not? When all was over, the coachman carefully descended the hill. He had come hither in haste, wishing to witness the sport himself; but now he drove slowly, and indulged in every sort of roundabout to spin out his time and our money. We met with a friend who, on our complaint, expostulated with him, and said,— "Señor, these gentlemen say that you drive them very slowly (*muy poco á poco*)." To the which he,—"Señor, if gentlemen will hire a carriage by the hour, and not by the afternoon, they must expect to get on very softly."—*Mem.* A white driver is always addressed as *Señor*, and I have occasionally heard such monologues as the following:—"Señor, why do you drive me this way? Curse you, Señor! You don't know anything, Señor! You are the greatest ass I ever encountered." The coachman takes it all coolly enough; the "Señor" spares his dignity, and he keeps his feelings to himself.

The writer of this has already spoken of various disappointments, in the way of seeing things, incidental to the position of the sex in Cuba. She came abroad prepared for microscopic, telescopic, and stereoscopic investigation,—but, hedged in on all sides by custom and convenience, she often observed only four very bare walls and two or three very stupid people. What could she see? Prisons? No. Men naked and filthy, lying about, using very unedifying language, and totally unaccustomed to the presence of Lady-visitors. She invoked the memory of Mrs. Fry and the example of Miss Dix. "Oh, they were saints, you know." "Only because they went to prisons, which you won't let me do."—Bull-fight? No. "How could you go back to Boston after seeing a bull-fight, eh?" "As if married life were anything else, eh?" And so on.—Negro ball? "Not exactly the place for a lady." "Miss Bremer went." "Very differently behaved woman from you." "Yes, virtue with a nose, impregnable."

But there is something she can go to see,—at least, some one,—the angelic man, Don Pepe, the wise, the gentle, the fearless, whom all the good praise. Yes, she shall go to see Don Pepe; and one burning Sunday noon she makes a pilgrimage through the scorching streets, and comes where he may be inquired for, and is shown up a pair of stairs, at the head of which stands the angelic man, mild and bland, with great, dark eyes, and a gracious countenance. He ushers us into a room furnished with nothing but books, and finds two chairs for us and one for himself, not without research.

Now I will not pretend to say that Don Pepe occupied himself with me after the first kind greeting, nor that my presence occasioned him either pleasure or surprise. My companion was a man after his own heart, and, at first sight, the two mounted their humanitarian hobbies, and rode them till they were tired. And when this time came, I went away and said nothing. Yet I knew that I had seen a remarkable man.

Don Pepe de la Luz is a Cuban by birth, and his age may number some sixty years. He inherited wealth and its advantages, having received somewhere a first-rate education, to which he has copiously added in subsequent years. He is a Liberal in politics and religion, a man of great reason and of great heart. In affairs of state, however, he meddles not, but contents himself with making statesmen. Like all wise Philanthropists, he sees the chief source of good to man in education, and devotes his life, and in a degree, his fortune, to this object. The building in which we found him was a large school, or rather college, founded by himself, and carried on in a great measure through his efforts. This college is upon the same literary footing as the University of Havana; and Don Pepe's graduates pass examinations and receive diplomas in the last-named institution. He himself rarely leaves its walls; and though he has house and wife elsewhere, and the great world is everywhere open to him, he leads here a more congenial life of ascetic seclusion, study, and simplicity.

"Oh, noble instinct of good men, to stay and do their duty!

This let us celebrate above all daring, wit, and beauty."

Don Pepe has been abroad as much as it profits a man to be,—but has not lost his own soul there, as an American is apt to do. He has known the best men in Europe and America. The best languages, he possesses them; the best books, here they are, piled all about his room. The floor is carpeted with them; there are cases all around the walls; and a large parallelogramic arrangement in the middle of the room, stuck all with books, as a pincushion with pins. True, there is not in their arrangement that ornateness of order observable in Northern libraries; dust even lies and blows about; and though he can find his favorites, *we* should be much puzzled to find any volume where it ought to be. But it looks as if the master were happy and undisturbed here, and as if the housemaid and her hated broom were as far off as the snow and frost.

In person, Don Pepe is not above the middle height. He is a fairly developed man, but looks thin and worn, and his shoulders have the stoop of age, which scholars mostly anticipate. His face is much corrugated, but it bears the traces of vivacious thought and emotion, not the withering print of passion. Of his eyes I have already spoken; they are wise, kind, and full of Southern fire.

Don Pepe has had some annoyances from the government,—probably in the more sanguine period of his life. The experience of years has taught him the secret of living peaceably with all men. He can be great and good himself, without perpetually quarrelling with those who can be neither. He spoke with warm interest of his scholars. "They have much capacity," he said; "but we want a little more of that *air* you spoke of just now, Doctor." That air was Liberty. Reader, have you ever been in a place where her name was contraband? All such places are alike. Here, as in Rome, men who have thoughts disguise them; and painful circumlocution conveys the meaning of friend to friend. For treachery lies hid, like the scorpion, under your pillow, and your most trusted companion will betray your head, to save his own. I am told that this sub-treason reached, in the days of the Lopez invasion, an incredible point. After every secret meeting of those affected to the invaders, each conspirator ran to save himself by denouncing all the others. One Cuban, of large fortune and small reputation, being implicated in these matters, brought General Concha a list of all his confederates, which Concha burned before his face, unread. Piteous, laughable spectacle! Better be monkeys than such men; yet such work does Absolutism in government and religion make of the noble human creature! God preserve us ever from tyrants, spies, and Jesuits!

Don Pepe does not tell us this; but we have much pleasant talk with him about books, about great men in Europe, and lastly about Prescott, whom he knew and honored. We took leave of him with regret. He accompanied us to the head of the stairs, and then said, "Ah! my dear Madam, my liver will not suffer me to go down." "I am glad it is not your heart," I rejoined, and we parted,—to meet again, in my thoughts, and perhaps elsewhere, in the dim vista of the future.

CHAPTER XII.

MATANZAS.

A HOT and dusty journey of some six hours brought us to Matanzas at high noon. Our companions were Cubans, Spaniards, Americans, and game-chickens, who travel extensively in these parts, sometimes in little baskets, with openings for the head and tail, sometimes in the hands of their owners, secured only by a string fastened to one foot and passed over the body. They seem to be objects of tender solicitude to those who carry them; they are nursed and fondled like children, and at intervals are visited all round by a negro, who fills his mouth with water, and squirts it into their eyes and under their feathers. They are curiously plucked on the back and about the tail, where only the long tail-feathers are allowed to grow. Their tameness in the hands of their masters is quite remarkable; they suffer themselves to be turned and held in any direction. But when set down, at any stage of the journey, they stamp their little feet, stretch their necks, crow, and look about them for the other cock with most belligerent eyes. As we have said that the negro of the North is an ideal negro, so we must say that the game-cock of Cuba is an ideal chicken, a fowl that is too good to be killed,—clever enough to fight for people who are too indolent and perhaps too cowardly to fight for themselves,—in short, the Gladiator of the Tropics.

Well, as we have said, we and they arrived at our journey's end in the extreme heat of the day; and having shown our paper and demanded our trunks, we beat an instantaneous retreat before the victorious Monarch of the skies, and lo! the Ensor House, dirty, bare, and comfortless, was to us as a fortress and a rock of defence.

Here I would gladly pause, and giving vent to my feelings, say how lovely I found Matanzas. But ever since Byron's time, the author is always hearing the public say, "Don't be poetical," etc., etc.; and in these days both writer and reader seem to have discovered that life is too short for long descriptions,—so that when the pen of a G. P. R. James, waiting for the inspirations of its master, has amused itself with sketching a greater or less extent of natural scenery, the rule of the novel-reader is invariably, "Skip landscape, etc., to event on thirty-second page." Nevertheless, I will say that Matanzas is lovely,—with the fair harbor on one hand and the fair hills on the other, sitting like a mother between two beautiful daughters, who looks from one to the other and wonders which she loves best. The air from the water is cool and refreshing, the sky is clear and open, and the country around seems to beckon one to the green bosom of its shades. "Oh, what a relief after Havana!" one says, drawing a full breath, and remembering with a shudder the sickening puffs from its stirring streets, which make you think that Polonius lies unburied in every house, and that you nose him as you *knows* not, as you pass the door and window-gratings. With this exclamation and remembrance, you lower yourself into one of Mr. Ensor's rocking-chairs,—twelve of which, with a rickety table and a piano, four crimson tidies and six white ones, form the furniture of the Ensor drawing-room,—you lean your head on your hand, close your eyes, and wish for a comfortable room with a bed in it. A tolerable room you shall have; but for a bed, only a cot-bedstead with a sacking bottom,—further, nothing. Now, if you are some folks that I know, you will be able to establish very comfortable repose on this slender foundation, Nature having so amply furnished you that you are your own feather-bed, bolster, sofa-cushion, and easy-chair, a moving mass of upholstery, wanting only a frame to be set down in and supported. But if you should be one of Boston's normal skeletons, pinched in every member with dyspepsia, and with the mark of the beast Neuralgia on your forehead, then your skin will have a weary time of it, holding your bones, and you will be fain to entreat with tears the merciful mediation of a mattress.

Now I know very well that those of my readers who intend visiting Cuba will be much more interested in statistics of hotels than in any speculations, poetical or philosophical, with which I might be glad to recompense their patience. Let me tell them, therefore, that the Ensor House is neither better nor worse than other American hotels in Cuba. The rooms are not very bad, the attendance not intolerable, the table almost commendable. The tripe, salt-fish, and plantains were, methought, much as at other places. There were stews of meat, onions, sweet peppers, and *ochra*, which deserve notice. The early coffee was punctual; the tea, for a wonder, black and hot. True, it was served on a bare pine table, with the accompaniment only of a bit of dry bread,—no butter, cake, nor *dulces*. But Mr. Ensor has heard, no doubt, that sweet things are unwholesome, and is determined, at whatever cost to his own feelings, to keep them out of the way of his guests, who are, for the time, his children. Then there is an excellent English servant called John, whom, though the fair Ensor did berate him, we must enumerate among the comforts of the establishment. There is a dark corner about *volantes*, which they are disposed to order for you at a very unreasonable profit; but as there are plenty of livery stables at hand, and street *volantes* passing all the time, it will be your own fault if you pay six dollars where you ought to pay three.

The first thing to be done at Matanzas is to drive out and see the Cumbre, a hill in the neighborhood, and from it the valley of the Yumori. The road is an improvement on those already described;—the ruts being much deeper and the rocks much larger, the jolting is altogether more complete and effective. Still, you remember the doctrine that the *volante* cannot upset, and this blind faith to which you cling carries you through triumphantly. The

Cumbre is lofty, the view extensive, and the valley lovely, of a soft, light green, like the early leaves and grass of spring, dotted everywhere with the palms and their dark clusters. It opens far, far down at your feet, and on your left you see the harbor quiet and bright in the afternoon sun, with a cheering display of masts and pennons. You would look and linger long, but that the light will wane, and you are on your way to Jenks his sugar-plantation, the only one within convenient distance of the town. Here the people are obviously accustomed to receive visitors, and are decently, not superfluously, civil. The *major-domo* hands you over to a negro who speaks English, and who salutes you at once with, "Good-bye, Sir!" The boiling here is conducted in one huge, open vat. A cup and saucer are brought for you to taste the juice, which is dipped out of the boiling vat for your service. It is very like balm-tea, unduly sweetened; and after a hot sip or so you return the cup with thanks. A loud noise, as of cracking of whips and of hurrahs, guides you to the sugar-mill, where the crushing of the cane goes on in the jolliest fashion. The building is octagonal and open. Its chief feature is a very large horizontal wheel, which turns the smaller ones that grind the cane. This wheel is turned after the following manner. In the centre of the building, and as it were in the second story, stands a stout post, to which are attached, at equal distances, six horizontal bars, which are dragged round by six horses, vehemently flogged by the like number of slaves, male and female. This is really a novel and picturesque sight. Each negro is armed with a short whip, and their attitudes, as they stand, well-balanced on the revolving wheel, are rather striking. Liberal as they were of blows and of objurations to the horses, all their cries and whipping produced scarcely a tenth of the labor so silently performed by the invisible, noiseless slave that works the steam-engine. From this we wandered about the avenues, planted with palms, cocoas, and manifold fruit-trees,—visited the sugar-fields, where many slaves were cutting the canes and piling them on enormous ox-carts, and came at last to a great, open field, where many head of cattle were quietly standing. Our negro guide had not been very lavish or intelligible in his answers to our numerous questions. We asked him about these cattle. "Dey cows," he replied. We asked if they gave milk, and if butter was made on the plantation. He seemed quite puzzled and confused, and finally exclaimed,—"*Dat cows no got none wife.*" Coming nearer, we found that the cows were draught oxen, employed in dragging the canes and other produce of the plantation. Jenks his garden we found in good order, and beautiful with many plants in full blossom; but Jenks his house seemed dreary and desolate, with no books, a wretched print or so, dilapidated furniture, and beds that looked like the very essence of nightmare. Nothing suggested domestic life or social enjoyment, or anything ———; but as Jenks is perfectly unknown to us, either by appearance or reputation, we give only a guess in the dark, and would suggest, in case it may displease him, that he should refurnish and repaint a little, and diffuse an air of cheerfulness over his solitary villa, remembering that Americans have imaginations, and that visitors will be very apt to construct an unknown host from his surroundings.

The second thing to be done in Matanzas, if you arrive on Saturday, is to attend military mass at the Cathedral on Sunday morning. This commences at eight o'clock; but the hour previous may be advantageously employed in watching the arrival and arrangement of the female aristocracy of Matanzas. These enter in groups of twos and threes, carrying their prayer-books, and followed by slaves of either sex, who bear the prayer-carpet of their mistresses. The ladies are wonderfully got up, considering the early hour; and their toilettes suggest that they may not have undressed since the ball of the night before. All that hoops, powder, and puffery can do for them has been done; they walk in silk attire, and their hair is what is technically termed dressed. Some of them bring their children, bedizened like dolls, and mimicking mamma's gestures and genuflection in a manner more provoking to sadness than to satire. If the dressing is elaborate, the crossing is also. It does not consist of one simple cross, "*in nomine Patris*," etc.; they seem to make three or four crosses from forehead to chin, and conclude by kissing the thumb-nail, in honor of what or whom we could not imagine. Entering the middle aisle, which is divided from the rest by a row of seats on either side, they choose their position, and motion to the dark attendant to spread the carpet. Some of them evince considerable strategic skill in the selection of their ground. All being now in readiness, they drop on their knees, spread their flounces, cross themselves, open their books, and look about them. Their attendants retire a little, spread a handkerchief on the ground, and modestly kneel behind them, obviously expecting to be saved with the family. These are neatly, sometimes handsomely dressed. In this *status* things remain until the music of the regiment is heard. With a martial sound of trumpets it enters the church, and fills the aisles, the officers taking place within the chancel, and a guard of honor of eight soldiers ranging on either side of the officiating priest. And now our devotions begin in good earnest; for, simultaneously with the regiment, the *jeunessé dorée* of Matanzas has made its appearance, and has ranged itself along the two long lines of demarcation which separate the fair penitents from the rest of the congregation. The ladies now spread their flounces again, and their eyes find other occupation than the dreary Latin of their missals. There is, so to speak, a lively and refreshing time between the youths of both sexes, while the band plays its utmost, and *Evangel*, *Kyrie*, and *Credo* are recited to the music of Trovatore and Traviata. That child of four years old, dressed in white and gold flounces, and white satin boots with heels, handles her veil and uses her eyes like Mamma, eager for notice, and delighted with the gay music and uniforms. The moment comes to elevate the Host,—thump goes the drum, the guard presents arms, and the soldiers, instead of kneeling, bend forward, in a most uncomfortable manner. Another thump, and all that is over; the swords are returned to their sheaths, and soon, the loud music coming to an end, the regiment marches out of church, very much as it marched in, its devotional experiences being known to Heaven alone. Ladies and lovers look their last, the flounces rise in pyramids, the prayer-carpets are rolled up, and with a silken sweep and rush, Youth, Beauty, and Fashion forsake the church, where Piety has hardly been, and go home to breakfast. To that comfortable meal you also betake yourself, musing on the small heads and villanous low foreheads of the Spanish soldiery, and wondering how long it would take a handful of resolute Yankees to knock them all into—— But you are not a Filibuster, you know.

CHAPTER XIII.

THE PASEO—THE PLAZA—DINING OUT.

"As this Sunday is Carnival, you cannot do better than drive about the city, and then go to the Plaza to see the masks. My partner's wife, with whom you have now so comfortably breakfasted, will call for you in her *volante* this afternoon, between five and six o'clock. She will show you the Paseo, and we will go and see the masks afterwards."

So spoke a banker, who, though not *our* banker, is our friend, and whose kind attentions we shall ever recall, when we remember Cuba. So he spoke, and so it befell. The pretty American lady, Cubanized into paleness, but not into sallowness, called at the appointed hour, and in her company we visited the principal streets, and the favorite drive of the Matanzasts. The Paseo is shorter than that of Havana, but much prettier. We found it gay with *volantes*, whose fair occupants kept up an incessant bowing and smiling to their friends in carriages and on horseback. The Cubans are generally good riders, and their saddle-horses have the easiest and pleasantest gait imaginable. The heat of the climate does not allow the severe exercise of trot and gallop, and so these creatures go along as smoothly and easily as the waves of the sea, and are much better broken to obedience. The ladies of Matanzas seem to possess a great deal of beauty, but they abuse the privilege of powder, and whiten themselves with *cascarilla* to a degree that is positively ghastly. This *cascarilla* is formed by the trituration of egg-shells; and the oval faces whitened with it resemble a larger egg, with features drawn on it in black and red. In spite of this, they are handsome; but one feels a natural desire to rush in amongst them with a feather duster, and lay about one a little, before giving an available opinion of their good looks.

If the Paseo was gay, the streets of the city were gay also; the windows filled with faces and figures in full dress, with little groups of children at the feet of the grown people, like the two world-famous cherubs at the feet of the Madonna di San Sisto. There were crowds of promenaders too, everywhere, interspersed with parties of maskers, who went about screaming at the public with high, shrill voices. Leaving the *volante*, we descend to the Plaza, where is now the height and centre of movement, we find it flanked on all sides with little movable kitchens, where good things are cooked, and with tables, where they are sold and eaten. Fried cakes, fish, and meats seem the predominant bill of fare, with wine, coffee, and fruits. The masks are circulating with great animation; men in women's clothes, white people disguised as negroes, and negroes disguised as whites, prodigious noses, impossible chins and foreheads; the stream of popular fancy ran chiefly in these channels. We met processions consisting of a man carrying a rat in a cage, and shouting out, "Catch this rat!" followed by a perfect stampede of wild creatures, all yelling, "Catch that rat!" at the top of their voices. The twanging of the guitar is heard everywhere, accompanied by the high nasal voices of the natives, in various strains of monotony. In some spots the music is more lively, accompanied by the shaking of a gourd filled with dry seeds, which is called *ghirra*, and whose "chick-a-chick, chick-chick" takes the place of the more poetical castanets;—here you find one or more couples exhibiting their skill in Cuban dances, with a great deal of applause and chattering from the crowd around. Beside those of the populace, many aristocratic groups parade the Plaza, in full dress, crowned with flowers and jewels;—a more motley scene can hardly be imagined. Looking up, one sees in curious contrast the tall palms with which the Plaza is planted, and the quiet, wondering stars set in the deep tropical heavens.

But in our evening's programme, tea has been omitted; now, what availeth a Bostonian without his tea? By eight o'clock, we are pensive, "most like a tired child at a show,"—by half-past eight, stupid,—by nine, furious. Two hours of folly, taken on an empty stomach, alarm us for our constitution. A visit to the *café* is suggested and adopted. It proves to be crowded with people in fancy attire, who have laid aside their masks to indulge in beer, orgeat, and sherbet. While our Cuban friends regale themselves with sour-sop and *zapote* ice sweetened with brown sugar, we call for a cup of delicious Spanish chocolate, which is served with a buttered toasted roll, worthy of all imitation. Oh, how much comfort is in a little cup of chocolate! what an underpinning does it afford our spiritual house, a material basis for our mental operations! In its support, we go it a little longer on the Plaza, see more masks, hear more guitars and "catch this rat!" and finally return, in a hired *volante*, to the Ensor House, where rest and the bedless cots await us.

But we have friends in Matanzas, real born Cubans, who will not suffer us to remain forever in the Ensor House. They send their *volante* for us, one day, and we visit them. Their house, of the inevitable Cuban pattern, is richly furnished; the marbles of the floor are pure and smooth, the rug ample and velvety; the wainscoting of the walls, so to speak, is in handsome tiling,—not in mean, washy painting; the cane chairs and sofas are fresh and elegant, and there is a fine Erard piano. The Master of the house is confined to his room by illness, but will be happy to see us. His son and daughters speak English with fluency. They inform us, that the epidemic colds which prevail in Cuban winters are always called by the name of some recent untoward occurrence, and that their father, who suffers from severe influenza, has got the President's Message. We find Don José in a bedroom darkened by the necessary closing of the shutters, there being no other way of excluding the air. The bedsteads are of gilded iron, with luxurious bedding and spotless mosquito-nettings. His head is tied up with a silk handkerchief. He rises from his rocking-chair, receives us with great urbanity, and expresses his appreciation of the American nation and their country, which he himself has visited. After a short interview we leave him, but not until he has placed his house and all it contains "*á la disposition de Usted.*" We are then shown the pretty bedroom of the young ladies, whose toilettes are furnished in silver, the bath lined with tiling, the study, and the dining-room, where luncheon awaits us. We take leave, with a kind invitation to return and dine the next day, which, upon mature deliberation, we accept.

The *volante* comes for us next day, with Roqué, brightest of all living *caleseros*, fixed in his boots and saddle. After a pleasant drive we attain the house, and are received by its hospitable inmates as before. The interval before dinner, a tolerably long one, is filled up by pleasant chitchat, chiefly in English. The lady of the house does not, however, profess our vernacular, and to her understanding we lay siege in French, Italian, and laughter-provoking Spanish. Before dining we pay a second visit to the host, who is still busy digesting the President's Message. Obviously, the longer he has it under consideration, the worse he finds it. He has nausea from its bragging, his head aches with its loudness, and its emptiness fills him with wind. We are at our wits' end to prescribe for him, and take our leave with grave commiseration, telling him that we too have had it, but that the symptoms it produces in the North are a reddening in the cheek and a spasmodic contraction of the right arm. Now comes great dinner on. A slave announces it, and with as little ceremony as may be we take our places. And here we must confess that our friend the banker had rendered us an important service. For he had said,— "Look not upon the soup when it is hot, neither let any victuals entice thee to more than a slight and temporary participation; for the dishes at a Cuban dinner be many, and the guest must taste of all that is presented; wherefore, if he indulge in one dish to his special delectation, he shall surely die before the end." And it came to pass that we remembered this, and walked through the dinner as on egg-shells, gratifying curiosity on the one hand, and avoiding satiety on the other; with the fear of fulness, as it were, before our eyes. For oh, my friends! what pang is comparable to too much dinner, save the distress of being refused by a young woman, or the comfortless sensation, in times of economy, of having paid away a five-dollar gold piece in place of a silver quarter of a dollar?

But you, Reader, would like more circumstantiality in the account of this dinner, which united many perfections. It was handsome, but not splendid,— orderly, but not stately,—succulent, but not unctuous. It kept the word of promise to the smell and did not break it to the taste. It was a dinner such as we shall wish only to our best friends, not to those acquaintances who ask how we do when they meet us, and wish we were dead before we part. As for particulars, we should be glad to impart much useful information and many choice receipts; but the transitory nature of such an entertainment does not allow one to improve it as one could wish. One feature we remember, which is that the whole dinner was placed on the table at once, and so you had the advantage of seeing your work cut out before you. None of that hope deferred, when, after being worried through a dozen stews and *entrées*, you are rewarded at last with an infinitesimal fragment of the *rôti*. Nor, on the other hand, the unwelcome surprise of three supplementary courses and a dessert, when you have already dined to repletion, and feel yourself at peace with all the world. Here all was fair play; you knew what to expect and what was expected of you. Soup, of course, came first,—then fish,—then meat stewed with potatoes and onions,—then other meat with *ochra* and tomatoes,—then boiled chicken, which is eaten with a *pilaff* of rice colored with saffron,—then delicious sweet potatoes, yams, plantains, and vegetables of every sort,—then a kind of pepper brought, we think, from the East Indies, and intensely tropical in its taste,—then a splendid roast turkey, and ham strewed with small colored sugar-plums,—then —— well, is not that enough for one person to have eaten at a stretch, and that person accustomed to a Boston diet? Then came such a display of sweetmeats as would exercise the mind of a New England housekeeper beyond all power of repose,—a pudding,—a huge tart with very thick crust,—cakes of *yuca*,—a dish of cocoa-nut, made into a sort of impalpable preserve, with eggs and sugar,—then a course of fruits,—then coffee, of the finest quality, from the host's own plantation,—and then we arose and went into the drawing-room, with a thankful recollection of what we had had, and also a thankful assurance that we should have no more.

A drive by moonlight was now proposed, to see the streets and the masks, it being still Carnival. So the *volante* was summoned, with its smiling, silent Roqué, and the pretty daughter of the house took seat beside us. The streets around the Plaza proved quite impassable from the crowd, whose wild movements and wilder voices went nigh to scaring the well-trained horses. The little lady was accustomed, apparently, to direct every movement of her charioteer, and her orders were uttered in a voice high and sweet as a bird-call. "*Dobla al derecho, Roqué! Roqué, dobla al derecho!*" Why did not Roqué go mad, and exclaim,—"Yes, Señorita, and to heaven itself, if you bid me so prettily!" But Roqué only doubled as he was bid, and took us hither and thither, and back to the nest of his lady-bird, where we left her and the others with grateful regrets, and finally back to the Ensor House, which on this occasion seemed to us the end of all things.

CHAPTER XIV.

GAME-CHICKENS—DON RODRIGUEZ—DAY ON THE PLANTATION—DEPARTURE.

As there are prejudices in Cuba and elsewhere, touching the appropriate sphere of woman, Hulia was not taken to the Cockpit, as she had demanded and expected,—not to see the chickens fight, but to see the Spaniards see it.

Forgive her, ye Woman's-Righters, if on this occasion she was weak and obedient! You would have gone, no doubt,—those of you who have not husbands; but such as have must know how much easier it is to deal with the article man in his theoretical than in his real presence. You may succeed in showing by every convincement that you are his natural master and superior, and that there is every reason on earth why you should command and direct him. "No!——," says the wretch, shaking his fist, or shrugging his shoulders; and whatever your intimate convictions may be, the end is, that you do not.

Propitiated by that ready obedience which is safest, dear Sisters, in these contingencies, the proprietor of Hulia takes her, one morning, to see the establishment of a man of fortune in the neighborhood, where one hundred and forty game-chickens are kept for training and fighting. These chickens occupy two good-sized rooms, whose walls are entirely covered with compartments, some two feet square, in each of which resides a cock, with his little perch and drinking-vessel. They are kept on allowance of water and of food, lest they should get beyond fighting weight. Their voices are uplifted all day long, and on all moonlight nights. An old woman receives us, and conducts us to the training-pit, pointing out on the way the heroes of various battles, and telling us that this cock and the other have won *mucho dinero*, "much money." Each has also its appointed value;—this cock is worth forty dollars, this four ounces, this one six ounces,—oh, he is a splendid fellow! No periodal and sporadic hen-fever prevails here, but the *gallo-mania* is the chronic madness of the tropics.

The training-pit is a circular space inclosed with boards, perhaps some twelve feet in diameter. Here we find the proprietor, Don Manuel Rodriguez, with a negro assistant, up to the ears in business. Don Manuel is young, handsome, and vivacious, and with an air of good family that astonishes us. He receives us with courtesy, finds nothing unusual in the visit of a lady, but is too much engrossed with his occupation to accord us more than a passing notice. This is exactly as we could wish,—it allows us to study the Don, so to speak, *au naturel*. He is engaged at first in weighing two cocks, with a view to their subsequent fighting. Having ascertained their precise weight, which he registers in his pocket-memorandum, he proceeds to bind strips of linen around their formidable spurs, that in their training they may not injure each other with them. This being accomplished,—he all the while delivering himself with great volubility to his black Second,—the two cocks are taken into the arena; one is let loose there; the negro holds the other, and knocks the free fowl about the head with it. Sufficient provocation having been given, they are allowed to go at each other in their own fashion, and their attacks and breathing-spells are not very unlike a bout of fencing. They flap, fly at each other, fly over, peck, seize by the neck, let go, rest a moment, and begin again, getting more and more excited with each round. The negro separates them, when about to draw blood. And as for Don Manuel, he goes mad over them, like an Italian *maestro* over his favorite pupil. "*Hombre, hombre!*" he cries to the negro, "what a cock! By Heaven, what a couple! *Ave María santísima!* did one ever see such spirit? *Santísima Trinidad!* is there such fighting in all Matanzas?" Having got pretty well through with the calendar of the saints, he takes out his watch;—the fight has lasted long enough. One of the champions retires to take a little repose; another is brought in his place; the negro takes him, and boxes him about the ears of the remaining fowl,— brushing him above his head, and underneath, and on his back, to accustom him to every method of attack. Don Manuel informs us that the cock made use of in this way is the father of the other, and exclaims, with an air of mock compassion, *Pobre padre!* "Poor father!" The exercise being concluded, he takes a small feather, and cleans out therewith the throat of either chicken, which proves to be full of the sand of the arena, and which he calls *porquería*, "dirt."

We leave Don Manuel about to employ himself with other cocks, and, as before, too much absorbed to give our departure much notice. Strange to say, Hulia is so well satisfied with this rehearsal, that she expresses no further desire to witness the performance itself. We learn subsequently that Don Manuel is a man of excellent family and great wealth, who has lavished several fortunes on his favorite pursuit, and is hurrying along on the road to ruin as fast as chickens' wings can carry him. We were very sorry, but couldn't possibly interfere. Meantime, he appeared excessively jolly.

Our kind friends of the dinner were determined to pay us, in their persons, all the debts of hospitality the island might be supposed to contract towards strangers and Americans. Arrangements were accordingly made for us to pass our last day in Matanzas at a coffee-plantation of theirs, some four miles distant from town. They would send their travelling *volante* for us, they said, which was not so handsome as the city *volante*, but stronger, as it had need to be, for the roads. At eleven o'clock, on a very warm morning, this vehicle made its appearance at the door of the Ensor House, with Roqué in the saddle,—Roqué with that mysterious *calesero* face of his, knowing everything, but volunteering nothing until the word of command. Don Antoñico he tells us, has gone before on horseback;—we mount the *volante*, and follow. Roqué drives briskly at first, a slight breeze refreshes us, and we think the road better than is usual. But wait a bit, and we come to what seems an unworked quarry of coral rock, with no perceptible way over it, and Roqué still goes on, slowly indeed, but without stop or remark. The strong horses climb the rough and slippery rocks, dragging the strong *volante* after them. The *calesero* picks his way carefully; the carriage tips, jolts, and tumbles; the centre of gravity appears to be nowhere. The breeze dies away; the vertical sun seems to pin us through the head; we get drowsy, and dream of an uneasy sea of stones, whose harsh waves induce headache, if not sea-sickness. We wish for a photograph of the road;—first, to illustrate the inclusive meaning of the word; second, to serve as a remembrance, to reconcile us to all future highways.

Why these people are content to work out their road-tax by such sore travail of mind and body appeareth to us mysterious. The breaking of stone in state-prison is not harder work than riding over a Cuban road; yet this extreme of industry is endured by the Cubans from year to year, and from one human life to another, without complaint or effort. An hour or more of these and similar reflections brings us to a bit of smooth road, and then to the gate of the plantation, where a fine avenue of palms conducts us to the house. Here resides the relative and partner of our Matanzas friends, a man of intelligent and humane aspect, who comes to greet us, with his pleasant wife, and a pretty niece, their constant guest. The elder lady has made use of her retirement for the accomplishment of her mind. She has some knowledge of French and Italian, and, though unwilling to speak English, is able to translate from that language with entire fluency. The plantation-house is very pretty, situated just at the end of the palm-avenue, with all the flowers in sight,—for these are planted between the palms;—it has a deep piazza in front, and the first door opens into one large room, with sleeping-apartments on either side. Opposite this door is another, opening upon the court behind the house, and between the two our chairs are placed, courting the draught.—*N. B.* In Cuba, no one shuns a draught; you ride, drive, sit, and sleep in one, and, unless you are a Cuban, never take cold. The floor of this principal room is merely of clay rubbed with a red powder, which, mixed with water, hardens into a firm, polished surface. The house has but one story; the timbers of the roof, unwhitened, forming the only ceiling. The furniture consists of cane easy-chairs, a dining-table, and a pretty hammock, swung across one end of the room. Here we sit and talk long. Our host has many good books in French and Spanish,—and in English, Walter Scott's Novels, which his wife fully appreciates.

A walk is proposed, and we go first to visit *los negros chiquitos,—Anglicè,* "the small niggers," in their nursery. We find their cage airy enough; it is a house with a large piazza completely inclosed in coarse lattice-work, so that the *pequeñuelos* cannot tumble out, nor the nurses desert their charge. Our lady friend produces a key, unlocking a small gate which admits us. We found, as usual, the girls of eight and upwards tending the babies, and one elderly woman superintending them. On our arrival, African drums, formed of logs hollowed out, and covered with skin at the end, were produced. Two little girls proceeded to belabor these primitive instruments, and made a sort of rhythmic strumming, which kept time to a monotonous chant. Two other girls executed a dance to this, which, for its slowness, might be considered an African minuet. The dancing children were bright-looking, and not ungraceful. Work stops at noon for a recess; and the mothers run from the field to visit the imprisoned babies, whom they carry to their own homes and keep till the afternoon-hour for work comes round, which it does at two, P. M. We went next to the negro-houses, which are built, as we have described others, contiguous, in one hollow square. On this plantation the food of the negroes is cooked for them, and in the middle of the inclosed square stood the cooking-apparatus, with several large caldrons. Still, we found little fires in most of the houses, and the inmates employed in concocting some tidbit or other. A hole in the roof serves for a chimney, where there is one, but they as often have the fire just before their door. The slaves on this plantation looked in excellent condition, and had, on the whole, cheerful countenances. The good proportion of their increase showed that they were well treated, as on estates where they are overworked they increase scarcely or not at all. We found some of the men enjoying a nap between a board and a blanket. Most of the women seemed busy about their household operations. The time from twelve to two is given to the negroes, besides an hour or two after work in the evening, before they are locked up for the night. This time they improve mostly in planting and watering their little gardens, which are their only source of revenue. The negroes on this estate had formed a society amongst themselves for the accumulation of money; and our friend, the Manager of the plantation, told us that they had on his books two thousand dollars to their credit. One man alone had amassed six hundred dollars, a very considerable sum, under the circumstances. We visited also the house of the mayoral, or overseer, whose good face seemed in keeping with the general humane arrangements of the place,—as humane, at least, as the system permits. The negroes all over the island have Sunday for themselves; and on Sunday afternoons they hold their famous balls, which sometimes last until four o'clock on Monday morning. Much of the illness among the negroes is owing to their imprudence on these and like occasions. Pneumonia is the prevalent disease with them, as with the slaves in our own South; it is often acute and fatal. Everything in Cuba has such a tendency to go on horseback, that we could not forbear asking if dead men did, and were told that it was so,—the dead negroes being temporarily inclosed in a box, and conveyed to the cemetery on the back of a horse. Our friend, seeing our astonishment, laughed, and told us that the poor whites were very glad to borrow the burial-horse and box, to furnish their own funerals.

Dinner was served at four o'clock, quite informally, in the one sitting-room of the house. A black girl brushed off the flies with a paper fly-brush, and another waited on table. The dinner was excellent; but I have already given so many bills of fare in these letters, that I will content myself with mentioning the novelty of a Cuban country-dish, a sort of stew, composed of ham, beef, mutton, potatoes, sweet potatoes, *yuca*, and yams. This is called *Ayacco*, and is a characteristic dish, like eel-soup in Hamburg, or salt codfish in Boston;—as is usual in such cases, it is more relished by the inhabitants than by their visitors. On the present occasion, however, it was only one among many good things, which were made better by pleasant talk, and were succeeded by delicious fruits and coffee. After dinner we visited the vegetable garden, and the well, where we found Candido, the rich negro who had saved six hundred dollars, drawing water with the help of a blind mule. Now the Philanthrope of our party was also a Phrenologist, and had conceived a curiosity to inspect the head of the very superior negro who had made all this money; so at his request Candido was summoned from the well, and ordered to take off his hat. This being removed disclosed the covering of a cotton handkerchief, of which he was also obliged to divest himself. Candido was much too well bred to show any signs of contumacy; but the expression of his countenance varied, under the observation of the Phrenologist, from wonder to annoyance, and from that to the extreme of sullen, silent wrath. The reason was obvious,—he supposed himself brought up with a view to bargain and sale; and when informed that he had a good head, he looked much inclined to give somebody else a bad one. He was presently allowed to go back to his work; and our sympathies went with him, as it would probably take some days to efface from his mind the painful impression that he was to be sold, the last calamity that can happen to a negro who is in kind hands. We now wandered through the long avenues of palm and fruit trees with which the estate was planted, and saw the stout black wenches at their out-door occupations, which at this time consisted chiefly in raking and cleansing the ground about the roots of the trees and flowers. Their faces brightened as their employers passed, and the smaller children kissed hands. Returned to the house, we paused awhile to enjoy the evening red, for the sun was already below the horizon. Then came the *volante*, and with heartfelt thanks and regrets we suffered it to take us away.

And who had been the real hero of this day? Who but Roqué, fresh from town, with his experience of Carnival, and his own accounts of the masked ball, the Paseo, and the Señorita's beaux? All that durst followed him to the gate, and kissed hands after him. "*Adios, Roqué! Roqué, adios!*" resounded on all sides; and Roqué, the mysterious one, actually smiled in conscious superiority, as he nodded farewell, and galloped off, dragging us after him.

As we drove back to Matanzas in the moonlight, a sound of horses' feet made us aware that Don Antoñico, the young friend who had planned and accompanied our day's excursion, was to be our guard of honor on the lonely road. A body-servant accompanied him, like-wise mounted. Don Antoñico rode a milk-white Cuban pony, whose gait was soft, swift, and stealthy as that of a phantom horse. His master might have carried a brimming glass in either hand, without spilling a drop, or might have played chess, or written love-letters on his back, so smoothly did he tread the rough, stony road. All its pits and crags and jags, the pony made them all a straight line for his rider, whose unstirred figure and even speech made this quite discernible. For when a friend talks to you on the trot, much gulping doth impede his conversation,—and there is even a good deal of wallop in a young lady's gallop. But our friend's musical Spanish ran on like a brook with no stones in it, that merely talks to the moonlight for company. And such moonlight as it was that rained down upon us, except where the palm-trees spread their inverted parasols, and wouldn't let it! And such a glorification of all trees and shrubs, including the palm, which we are almost afraid to call again by name, lest it should grow "stuck up," and imagine there were no other trees but itself! And such a combination of tropical silence, warmth, and odor! Even in the night, we did not forget that the aloe-hedges had red in them, which made all the ways beautiful by day. Oh! it was what good Bostonians call "a lovely time"; and it was with a sigh of fulness that we set down the goblet of enjoyment, drained to the last drop, and getting, somehow, always sweeter towards the bottom.

For it was set down at the Ensor House, which we are to leave to-night, half-regretful at not having seen the scorpion by which we always expected to be bitten; for we had heard such accounts of it, patrolling the galleries with its venomous tail above its head, that we had thought a sight might be worth a bite. It was not to be, however. The luggage is brought; John is gratified with a *peso*; and we take leave with entire good-will.

I mention our departure, only because it was Cuban and characteristic. Returning by boat to Havana, we were obliged to be on board by ten o'clock that evening, the boat starting at eleven. Of course, the steamer was nowhere but a mile out in the stream; and a little cockle-shell of a row-boat was our only means of attaining her. How different, ye good New Yorkers and Bostonians, from your afternoon walk on board the "Bay State," with valise and umbrella in hand, and all the flesh-pots of Egypt in ——, well, in remembrance! After that degree of squabbling among the boatmen which serves to relieve the feelings of that habitually disappointed class of men, we chose our craft, and were rowed to the steamer, whose sides were steep and high out of water. The arrangements on board were peculiar. The body of the main deck was occupied by the *gentlemen's* cabin, which was large and luxurious. A tiny after-cabin was fitted up for the ladies. In the region of the machinery were six horrible staterooms, bare and dirty, the berths being furnished simply with cane-bottoms, a pillow, and one unclean sheet. Those who were decoyed into these staterooms endured them with disgust while the boat was at anchor; but when the paddle-wheels began to revolve, and dismal din of clang and bang and whirr came down about their ears, and threatened to unroof the fortress of the brain, why then they fled madly, precipitately, leaving their clothes mostly behind them. But I am anticipating. The passengers arrived and kept arriving; and we watched, leaning over the side, for Don Antoñico, who was to accompany our voyage. Each boat had its little light; and to see them dancing and toppling on the water was like a fairy scene. At last came our friend; and after a little talk and watching of the stars, we betook ourselves to rest.

Many of the Dons were by this time undressed, and smoking in their berths. As there was no access to the ladies' cabin, save through the larger one, she who went thither awaited a favorable moment and ran, looking neither to the right hand nor the left. The small cabin was tolerably filled by Cuban ladies in full dress.—*Mem.* They always travel in their best clothes.—The first navigation among them was a real balloon-voyage, with collisions; but they soon collapsed and went to bed. All is quiet now; and she of whom we write has thrown herself upon the first vacant bed, spreading first a clean napkin on the extremely serviceable pillow. Sleep comes; but what is this that murders sleep? A diminutive male official going to each berth, and arousing its fair occupant with "Doña Teresita," or whatever the name may be, "favor me with the amount of your passage-money." No comment is necessary; here, no tickets,—here, no Stewardess to mediate between the unseen Captain and the unprotected female! The sanctuary of the sex invaded at midnight, without apology and without rebuke! Think of that, *those* passengers who have not paid their fare, and, when invited to call at the Captain's office and settle, do so, and be thankful! The male passengers underwent a similar visitation. It is the Cuban idea of a compendious and economic arrangement.

And here ends our account of Matanzas, our journey thither, stay, and return. Peace rest upon the fair city! May the earthquake and hurricane spare it! May the hateful Spanish government sit lightly on its strong shoulders! May the Filibusters attack it with kisses, and conquer it with loving-kindness! So might it be with the whole Island—*vale*!

CHAPTER XV.

RETURN TO HAVANA—SAN ANTONIO AGAIN.

NOT many days did we tarry in Havana, on our return. We found the city hot, the hotel full, the invalids drooping. The heat and the confined life (many of them never crossed the threshold) began to tell upon them, and to undo the good work wrought by the mild winter. They talked of cooling breezes, and comfortable houses, with windows, carpets, and padded sofas. Home was become a sort of watchword among them, exchanged with a certain subdued rapture. One of them was on the brink of a longer journey. He had been the worst case all winter, and since our arrival, had rarely left his room. A friend was now come to take him to his father's house, but he failed so rapidly, that it was feared the slender thread would be broken before the sailing of the steamer should allow him to turn his face homewards. The charities of the Cubans, such as they are, do not extend to the bodies of dead Protestants,—for them is nothing but the Potter's Field. This gross Priest, that shameless woman shall lie in consecrated ground, but our poor countryman, pale and pure as he looked, would defile the sainted inclosure, and must be cast out, with dogs and heretics. So there was a sort of hush, even in the heartless hotel-life, and an anxious inquiry every morning,—"Is he yet alive?"

"Just alive," and for a moment, people were really interested. But the day of departure came at last, and he was carried on board in a chair, his coffin following him. His closed eyes were too weak to open on the glorious tropical noon, and take a last leave of its beauty, and of the dry land he was never to see again; for he died, we afterwards learned, the day before the vessel reached New York, without pain or consciousness. And many thus depart. In this very hotel died glorious Dr. Kane, having, like a few other illustrious men, compressed all the merits of a long life in the short years of youth. When he was carried from these walls, a great concourse rose up to attend him, and when the procession passed the Governor's palace, the dark Concha himself, the centre of power and despotism, stood at the gate, hat in hand, to do reverence to the noble corpse. A practical word àpropos of these things. A flight to the tropics is apt to be like a death-bed repentance, deferred to the last moment, and with no appreciable benefit. Not only giving,—everything is done twice which is done quickly,—Time and Disease having between them a ratio too mysterious and rapid for computation. Ye who must fly, wounded, from the terrible North, fly in season, before the wound festers and rankles,—otherwise you escape not, bringing Death with you. Do not rush moreover to a hotel in the heart of Havana, and falling down there, refuse to be removed. Pulmonary patients rarely profit in Havana, whose climate is tainted with the sea-board, and further, with all the abominations of the dirtiest of cities. Santa Cruz has a better climate than Cuba,—so has Nassau, but in Cuba there are better places than Havana. San Antonio is better,—Guines, Guanabacoa, even Matanzas, are all healthier. Best of all is to reside on a coffee or sugar-plantation in the interior, but to attain this object, special letters are necessary,—as before observed, neither *your* Banker, nor *our* Consul, will help you to it.

We find little news in Havana. B. has gone to Trinidad de Cuba,—C. has gone to New Orleans. The Bachelor who daily treated to oranges is among the departed, and remembering his benefactions, we wish him a safe return and continuance of celibacy. Carnival has been gay,—Concha gave a Ball, and our Consul plucked up heart and went, and introduced eight of our countrywomen, elegantly dressed, no doubt, and not speaking a word of Spanish, nor the Consul neither,—one of the requisites of an American foreign Official being that he shall be capable of no foreign language. This rule has been rigorously adhered to by the Administration for twenty years past, and in some instances, a tolerable ignorance of English has been added, as a merit of supererogation. However, to return to the Ball, one of the ladies performed in Boarding-school French, and as far as looks went, they made a decidedly good impression. The little English Lords are expected,—Ladies, do not flutter so!—it is not the fascinating English Lord who has glittered like a diamond for two years past on the finger of Washington diplomacy. These are Boys, and by all accounts, good ones.

There is an Englishman at the hotel already, and he quarrels with his victuals in a manner that is awful, quite reminding one of the stories of unthankful children, whom the wolves get. And he labors with the unknown Spanish like a ship at sea, and steers for this dish and that with undistinguishable orders. Though I know him not, I must help him when I see him struggling so for his dinner, winking, pointing, and sputtering to the waiters without result. The wretch has been in Italy, and would make the softer idiom serve his turn here. "*Riso, eh, riso, riz, rice,*" says he, with extended index. "*Trae el arroz al Señor*" comes timely to his aid, and with a few more helpings he is fed, though not satisfied. So irrational, so unappeasable is his appetite, that one cannot help thinking he has heard the story of the Belly and the Members in his youth, and has determined to avenge the injured ganglion of its ancient tormentors.

But among so many faces, remembered and sketched with little pleasure, there is one whose traits I must record as a labor of love. It belonged to one of the recent arrivals at the hotel, and was first seen in strong contrast with the countenance of the gluttonous Englishman, which it regarded with grave wonder. Expressive dark eyes, fine brows, heavy black hair, and a clear skin, subdued by ill-health, were its principal points of interest, but such enumeration can give you no more idea of its charm than an auctioneer's catalogue of furniture can suggest the features of a happy home. I had heard of its owner, but had never seen her before, yet we met somehow like people who had known each other, and a few commonplace phrases ended in a dialogue like this: "Are you A?"—"Yes,—are you B?"—"Yes;" and eternal friendship, though not sworn, set in immediately, and still perseveres. Modesty forbids us to praise our friend,—the very epithet "my friend," says the utmost we can say for any one. So I must not further celebrate my new-found treasure, who from this moment became the companion of all my steps in Cuba. I will only say that she was an apple-blossom of our Northern Spring, grafted upon a noble Southern stock, and turning her face now to the regions of the sun for healing warmth. Readers! you have all heard of her,—you would all give your ears to know her name. Keep them, you shall not.

In this pleasant company we sought San Antonio again. My friend was not doing well in Havana, and the graceful head was bowed every day lower by pain and weakness. But once out of the pent-up city, the head rose like a lily after rain, and all the little journey was pleasure and surprise. The tangled thickets, the new trees, the strange flowers, filled her with admiration. This was Cuba. Havana was, what is everywhere almost alike, the World. And soon we came to the clear, low-running river, with its green, bushy banks. And the next whistle of the steam-engine, like a fairy horn, called up the pretty village, with its streets and bridges, its one church, and its diminutive Plaza. We walk along the newly paved street, lined with small dwellings built of palm and plaster. The naked children are playing at the doors, the fathers and mothers are making cigars, or smoking them, the soldiers are walking vacantly about, and the small shopkeepers are looking out from behind their dull counters, piled with the refuse of the better markets. Here is the American Hotel, and just opposite, the eternal piano is playing "Norma," as it always did twelve hours out of twenty-four, and was a nuisance. But let me not grumble, for at the door of that house stand Mariquilla and Dolores, to welcome me back, and, hearing their voices, Norma leaves the instrument of her revenge, and comes out to embrace me. It is pleasant, is it not, to arrive where some one is glad to see you? These kind people quite warm my heart with their welcome. Mrs. L. at the hotel, too, is always glad to see a boarder, especially if he have with him a trunk that looks like staying. So we are fêted all around, and have the best rooms given us, and are happy.

In the evening, I betake myself to the house opposite, which was familiar to me in my earlier visit, but of which I now speak for the first time. Its inmates are in comfortable, though moderate circumstances, and their habits are the type of Cuban village-life. Here I meet the accustomed circle,—fie! they have no *circle*, but sit in two long parallel lines, and rock, and smoke at each other. Papa is a small, slight Spaniard, with good manners and no teeth. Mamma is not more than forty,—a massive, handsome woman, with that dignity of expression which is beyond beauty,—she is simple in her dress, and quiet in all her ways, but her thoughtful eyes make you remember her. Mariquilla is a buxom girl, some thirty years of age, who uses ten cosmetics in her bath, and still preserves a tolerably fresh complexion. Dolores is quiet and gentle, and spends her days in taking care of two little motherless children, whose father brings them every morning, and takes them away at night. Maria Luisa, whom I call Norma, is the only daughter of the family. She is pretty and modest, slight and small, like her father, but with fine eyes. She is a great Belle, we are told, in the neighborhood, and her musical accomplishment is considered prodigious. Besides these we find Dotor Hernandez, the village Physician, an Aragonese, thick-set and vigorous, with a good honest face, and Juanito, the Music-Master, a youth of eighteen, from Barcelona, with straight black hair, a pock-marked countenance, and a pair of as mischievous black eyes as ever looked demurely into the mysteries of the divine art. He is just offering cigarettes to all the family. Mamma has taken one, so have Dolores and Mariquilla,—he hands me the little packet with: "*Te fuma, Hulita?*" and seems rather surprised at my refusal, supposing doubtless that women of a certain age smoke, all over the world. One small lamp dimly illuminates this family party. When music is proposed, two candles, not of wax, are lighted, and placed on the piano. I sing a song or two, which they are good enough to call "*muy bonito*," and then, Maria Luisa, invited in turn, thunders through "Norma," from Overture to Finale. Oh! I have not described the piano,—it is a grand one, and bears the name of Stoddard. It should be about sixty years old, and would seem to have been through three generations and ten boarding-schools. It is a sort of skeleton piano, empty of music, and the rattling of its poor old bones makes mine ache. After the Opera, dancing is proposed. Juanito is disabled with a lame hand, and Maria Luisa volunteers to play the new *contra-danza*. It is christened "the Atlantic Telegraph," and is full of jerks and interruptions, having nothing very definite about it. We have learned the *contra-danza* of Dolores, on a former occasion, but now they all say "Hulita must dance with the Doctor," and to that consummate honor she resigns herself. That distinguished functionary divests himself of his cigar, polishes his perspiring forehead with his handkerchief, and offers himself as a candidate for her hand. "*Vamos*," he says, and they begin a slow, circling measure, to a music which is nondescript. Quiet work this, none of your spasmodic Waltzes, kicking Polkas, and teetotum jigmarigs. This gentle revolution seems imitated from the movement of the planets, or perhaps the dance of the seasons,—gravity pervades it,—it is a slow eternity. The rest of the family group has resolved itself into couples,—we all go round and round, and suddenly confront each other for a right and left, and look delighted, and then go round again. This dreamy performance goes on, until we have just sense enough left to remember that there is such a thing as bed-time. We break off, inquire the hour, find it late, say that we must go, which occasions no surprise. The piano ceases,—the candles are put out. There is a general kissing and "*Buenas noches, Hulita.*" Dotor Hernandez sees us home. We pass every evening at the house opposite, and all the evenings are like this.

CHAPTER XVI.

SAN ANTONIO—CHURCH ON SUNDAY—THE NORTHER—THE S. FAMILY.

THE least shrub has its blossom, if you only know how to find it. The dullest country town in New England has its days when people hear speeches and get drunk, the one act illustrating the morals, the other the manners of the community. In like manner, the smallest village in Cuba has its Sunday, when the imprisoned women go to church in their best clothes, the men attend cockfights, and in the evening there is ball or sermon, according as the Church makes feast or fast. The population of San Antonio does not seem particularly given to weekday devotion, nor indeed do you anywhere in Cuba find men and women praying in the churches, as you do in Rome. There is a degree of sobriety among the people in all things, partly Spanish, it may be, partly the result of the extreme climate,—certain it is, that the Cuban Spaniard has not, either in pleasure or devotion, the extravagance of the French or Italian. The church at San Antonio was always open, but I always found it empty, except on the one Sunday morning when I went thither to observe manners and customs. High mass was at eight o'clock, and was in all respects a miniature of the same ceremonial as described at Matanzas, the accompaniment of martial music and the regiment being left out. The body of the church was covered with prayer-carpets, which were closely occupied by kneeling figures. The display of good dresses and good looks was cheerful and invigorating. There was less flouncing and fanning, methought, than in the larger town; but no doubt the usual telegraphy was carried on, only in a more covert manner, as became the severer exigencies of village decorum. The priest went through his harmless little functions at the altar with what seemed to be a calico Dalmatique on his back, but we have no doubt that it was a brocade of creditable thickness. What he said was, of course, inaudible. Juanito was at the organ, perched sideways in a high gallery, so that his impish face and dancing eyes formed a part of the picture. Though nearer heaven in his position, he looked more full of the devil (pardon the expression) than we had ever seen him. With him were three young choristers, laboring away at the "Kyrie Eleison,"—he made the fourth in the Quartette, and played the accompaniment, too, losing, moreover, nothing of what went on below. The music was good, very like something of Mozart's, but when subsequently interrogated, Juanito declared it to have been a *Capriccio* of his own. We can only say, that if it was not Mozart's, we shall certainly hear of Juanito some day, as a composer.

The two old beggars who take off their tattered hats with such stately humility all the week, were here to-day, but did not beg in church. Item, they do not chatter like their Italian brethren in the trade, but commence a slow statement of their grievances, which you interrupt with "*nada*," nothing, when they walk sadly away. A Cuban generally gives them something, and always without rebuke. In the church was, too, a kneeling figure of Christ, neither divine nor human, fastened to a platform, with four lanterns at the four corners,—it is carried through the streets on Fridays in Lent for devotion, and the priests chant, and bear candles before it.

Well, Mass is over, and we walk back to the hotel,—and here is our pretty neighbor, Maria Luisa, watching at the door to see the people come from church. "What, not at Mass, Maria Luisa?" "No, I'm so sorry, but Papa is away, and Dolores has a cold, and Mariquilla has been sitting up with a sick friend, so there was no one to go with me." Clearly, there is a laxity in matters of religion in the house opposite. On the other hand public opinion, even in San Antonio, would never have permitted Maria Luisa, or any other female under sixty to have walked the quiet streets without escort, upon whatever errand of piety or of charity. Scarcely to the bedside of a dying mother might she go, unattended by a suitable companion. We pass the remainder of the Sunday in quiet resignation to the heat, the thermometer standing at 86 in the shade, (say, on the fourth of March,) and letter-writing causing one to perspire like a wood-sawyer, or a stout youth in the Polka. For the nobler sex, there is the cockpit,—all the *cafés* and billiards too are full of soldiers and countrymen,—one hears the click of the balls throughout the quiet streets. Towards sunset we walk out, and find the village alive with little groups of people, and the windows of the houses, at least the window-gratings, filled with the best women in the best dresses. Some of them are well got-up. All look cool, easy, and indolent. Here and there is seen amongst them the glimmer of a furtive cigar. We pass the Cavalry Barracks, once a spacious monastery, and see the horses gathered in from their wide pasture for the night. They obey the voice, and with a little driving, make a tolerable charge at the arched doorway, and carry it in style. The sense of smell too is regaled with the savory odors of the soldiers' supper, and looking in at a grating, we see huge stewpans simmering over charcoal fires,—the rest in darkness, for it now grows late. The men are a stouter looking set than the regiment we saw at Matanzas, but the horses have not the bone and muscle requisite for heavy action,—they could only make respectable light-horse. Returning home, we meet our friends of the house opposite going to "*Sermon*," as they tell us, for this is Lent, and not Carnival. Mamma wears a black veil,—the others are bareheaded. We have still tea to look forward to, but under such difficulties! we have given a dollar for a teapot which in Boston should cost twenty-five cents. Our precious pound of black tea, brought from home, has not yet given out, but how hard is it to make Antonio, the head-waiter, put the tea in the pot, make the water boil, and pour it boiling over the tea. Yet this sacred rite we accomplish every evening. It has the solemnity of a religious observance, for where the tea-table is, there is home. After tea, a chair by the well in the middle of the Court, and a silent feast of tropical starlight. The lady of the house is chattering nothings with that queer Californian, who looks as much like a spoiled preacher as anything. The excitable Carolinian has got some one to hear him abuse Cuba, and glorify Charleston. Yonder at the left angle the flare of a lamp betrays the kitchen, and in the next compartment of the picture Polonia, the slave washer-woman, who has been kept at the ironing-table all day, vents her feelings in passionate snatches of talk, shakes her kerchiefed head, tosses her arms about, and returns to the ironing with more determination than ever. Poor slave,—a great debt was piled up against her before she was born, and the labor of all her life cannot work it out. Bankrupt must she die, and hand down the debt, sole inheritance, to her children. So the world to the slave is a debtor's prison, with a good or bad Jailer, and for utmost alleviation, an occasional treat all round. And while the cooking, and chattering, and ironing goes on about us, Reader, you and I will ponder this, sitting by the well, under the stars set an hundred thousand miles deep in the dark velvet of the tropical heavens.

This was Sunday, and with the next day came one of those changes which resemble in kind, not in degree, the caprices of our own Continental climate. The day has been a little less genial than usual, still we are all comfortably seated at dinner, when a sudden wind shakes the house, and blowing in furiously at the blinds, threatens to make the tablecloth fly over our heads. A fierce shower of rain follows,—our table is set in a gallery inclosed on one side only with Venetian blind-work, and through this the rain rushes at us like a volley of canes flung into the pit of a theatre. It grows dark, and for an hour or so, very cold. There is an instantaneous closing of doors and wooden window-shutters, and we of the Dinner protect ourselves from the wet and chill with the few warm garments we have with us,—for is not the bulk of our solid clothing laid up at Havana in that sea-trunk which we could wish never to open again? We pass the remainder of the afternoon under hatches, as it were. The rain soon exhausts itself, but the cold wind continues for some days. This is the Norther, fatal to yellow fever, but fatal also to those who are ill of it, and dreaded by all patients whatever. To us, the storm being over, the wind is only chilly, bringing with it a dull sky, and the desire for exercise, but the invalids shrivel up in it like rose-leaves in a frost,—the hectic gives place to deadly pallor, and the purple hues that mark the orbit of the eye come out, stronger than ever. Meeting, they interrogate each other's faces with anxious looks, as if wishing to see what headway their little community could keep against the common foe. The aspect of the streets is changed. The women scarcely appear, save where you see the heads of three or four of them in a row, looking through the small square breathing-hole cut in the window-shutters, and giving one the idea of so many people standing erect in their coffins. The men walk moodily about, each one enveloped in the dark folds of a Spanish cloak, or *capa*, of which the material varies from fine to coarse, but the shape is always the same. These solemn, stalking figures so resemble the *mysterious personages* of the theatre, the bandits, spies, disguised lovers, and other varmint, that we saw for once where the stage has preserved a tradition of real life, these costumes having been, no doubt, long since imitated from Spain, and never changed.

What crime is this grave man meditating, with heavy brow and splendid eyes? Murder or conspiracy, at least. No, he only wants to purchase a string of onions at that shop at the corner. And this melancholy hero with the pale olive complexion, dark as the stage-Romeo after he has bought the poison? He enters yonder door to refresh himself with a glass of *aguardiente*, and a game of billiards. At the house opposite, Dolores complains of "*muchisima flussion*,"—a most severe cold. "Is it the President's Message?" we ask. "No, in San Antonio they call the cold '*el Polvorin*,' after the powder-magazine that exploded, last year, in Havana." We tell Dotor Hernandez that he must cure Dolores, and he promises her a "*vomitivo*" next morning, the very mention of which considerably hastens her convalescence. The health of the village is suffering from the Norther, the Doctor has his hands full. Mariquilla must give us some account of the sick friend she is nursing. "He has a *Calentura*, (fever of the country,) with delirium. They treat him with leeches, bleeding, borage tea, mustard at the feet; around the head bread with oil, vinegar, and pepper, as a *preventivo*." "Why," cried one of us, "you have seasoned him and stuffed him with herbs, fit for roasting." Dotor Hernandez gravely explains and defends his practice.

While the Norther is in full force, we go to pay a visit to Don Juan Sanchez, a man of wealth and position in San Antonio, and proprietor of large estates in the neighborhood. Don Juan is not at home,—his wife, Doña Tomasita, and the Tutor, an elderly Frenchman, receive us. She is young, but the mother of seven children. At our request, the nursery is reviewed in the parlor, as follows: Enter Manuel, eight years of age, enveloped in the stage cloak, and with the utmost gravity of countenance. He marches up to us, and startles us by inquiring after our health, in very good English. Enter Tomas Ignacio, seven years of age, also in a *capa*, and grave. This infant addressed us in French, and took a seat beside his brother. He was followed by two noble imps, of six and five, dressed in the same manner, and with the same decorum. These four creatures in linen suits, with black cloaks, were positively imposing, and it was not until Dolorita, the baby, had begun to howl in her mother's arms, and Ricardo, the three-year old, to tumble on the floor at her feet, that we could feel we were in the presence of lawless, spontaneous childhood. Before we departed, Doña Tomasita kindly placed her whole house, and all her earthly goods at our disposition, and we, with great moderation, claimed only the right of exit at her front door.

CHAPTER XVII.

EDUCATION—LAST NIGHT IN SAN ANTONIO—FAREWELL.

ONE of our number, visiting the public schools of San Antonio one day, found the course of studies for boys of very respectable extension,—it comprised all the usual elementary branches, including the History of Spain, such a history of that country at least as is good for Cuban boys to learn. For the education of girls, a single hour was reserved, and into this were crowded the necessary reading and writing, a little instruction in accounts, and the geography of the island. My friend remonstrated against this unequal division of the spoils of time, but those in authority insisted that it was according to the rights of Nature, as follows.

American. Do you mean to say that boys should be taught five or six hours a day, and girls only one?

Schoolmaster. Certainly.

American. Why do you make this difference?

Schoolmaster. Because women need so much less education than men.

American. Why is that?

Schoolmaster. They have less mind, in the first place, and then their mode of life demands less cultivation of what they have.

American. What knowledge do you consider necessary for a woman? only reading and writing, I suppose.

Schoolmaster. Yes, and a little arithmetic. They must fill up the rest of their time with sewing, and household matters.

American. But supposing you were required to add something to this small amount of instruction, what would it be?

Schoolmaster (after some reflection). I scarcely know, unless indeed *a slight coloring of Grammar.*

Our American, now excited, brings in view the good of the race. "Do you not think," he says, "that by elevating the organism of the mothers, you elevate the intellectual chances of the whole race? Stupid mothers will have stupid sons,—the results of culture are inherited."

The master replies that that is not his business, but Don Juan, who happens to be present, being appealed to, assents, and thinks it might be as well if a mother could have an idea. So far, so good, but a jealous-hearted woman to whom the conversation was reported smiled to observe how both American and Cuban made woman subservient to the interests of the race. "And if she should never be a mother," said this one, "educate her for herself, that she may give good counsel, and discern the noble and the beautiful. For women are good to inspire men, as well as to bear them, and for their own sakes, they have a right to know all that elevates and dignifies life." And this brings to mind another brief conversation overheard in one of our voyages.

Young Wife (holding up a number of the "Atlantic Monthly"). Ought women to learn the alphabet, dear? what do you think?

Young Husband. Oh! certainly—don't they have to teach it?

But the time draws nigh for us to leave San Antonio. Our return passages are engaged in the next Isabel. If this steamer prove such a Bird of Gladness as the papers and her consignees say, then our once weary voyage will become a veritable translation,—only three days of sunshine, smoothness, and turtle-soup for luncheon, and you land in Charleston in undisturbed equilibrium of manners and of dress. Well, more of this anon.

But to-night is our last night in San Antonio. We have danced our last *contra-danza* with Dotor Hernandez, and had our last chat with Maria Luisa and her mother. Juanito was there, that evening, and as we were all in a musical mood, he played through whole piano-forte arrangements of "Norma" and "Lucia," and we all screamed through the score, some six notes too high for the voice, Papa and Mamma applauding us, and did wonders in "Casta Diva" and "*Chi mi frena.*" But this is all at an end, and one of us stands alone at her open window, and looks for the last time on the quiet scene,—just before her is the little pasture where the goats pick up a scanty subsistence all day, and where shadows and moonlight play such wild freaks at night. This morning, as she sat at that window and worked, two men in haste carried a coffin past it. She always sees coffins, and sometimes writes about them,—that one gives tone to her thoughts to-night. For the house opposite is now dark and still,— the parlor where Mariquilla embroiders her chemises, and Dolores pulls lint for the sick is silent and deserted. The trees stand up there in the moonlight, and the river runs among its shallows so near that one hears its voice. And Hulita thinks: fifty years from this time—that river will be running just as it is now, and those trees, or others like them, will be standing at the angle of the picture as I now see them, but where shall we, friends of to-day, be? Dead, or old enough to die. Juanito will be a man in years, then, with white hairs, scarcely remembering the American lady who praised his compositions in church-music. The Dotor, Papa, and Mamma cannot be alive, Maria Luisa will be a Grandmother, and if Hulita lives, her infirmities will make death a welcome deliverance. So she envies that moon, the trees, the river, who can all stay and be eternal. She saw the coffin to-day,—very like she will see the whole no more. Good-night, dear moon, dear shadows, dear unlearned, unsophisticated people,—I shall leave you to-morrow, forget you never.

And the next day comes the bustle of departure, and packing of trunks, for we are to take the afternoon train down to Havana. Doña Tomasita sends a parting gift of fruit, as much as one man and one stout boy can carry. The fruit is as follows: one bushel of golden, honeyed oranges,—oh! the glory of all oranges are those of this island,—the same quantity of *chaimitos* and *mameys*, and a huge fagot of sugar-cane. We hasten to share these good creatures with those immediately at hand, having lauded Doña Tomasita to the skies and paid her messengers. What could be carried away we took with us. Then came the parting with Polonia, who wrung her hands as usual, and cried out: "Know thou, girl, that I shall miss thee much." "And I thee, too, thou dear old half-mad charcoal figure,—thou art human, though black, and canst ache over the ironing-table as well as another. Let these few reals console thee, as far as may be, for the loss of my sympathy. If we ever get the Island, I will help thee to ease and good wages.

"But not so to thee, roguish Antonio. 'Art thou not free and perfidious? We intrusted a sum of money to thine hand to pay the negro baggage-carrier, and to slightly fee thyself, and we ascertain all too late, by the complaints of the injured negro, that thou didst slightly fee him, and pay thyself for services never rendered. Wherefore dread our coming, or the Day of Justice, by whomsoever administered!'"——

We have taken affectionate leave of the family of the house opposite, promising to write, with the remainder of our mortal lives as the vague term of fulfilment. A trinket or two made the younger ones happy, while the whole family solemnly united to bestow on me a little set of vignettes of Cuba, folded fan-fashion, and purchasable for the sum of five reals. Not without much explanation was it delivered to me,—this was the Cock-fight, this the Bull-fight, this the Tacon theatre. I received these instructions without any of that American asperity which led a celebrated Chief Justice to say: "There are some things, Mr. Counsel, which the Court is supposed to know," and gratefully departed. We walked to the *dépôt*, in the hot afternoon sun, our smaller pieces conveyed on a barrow, and the huge trunk resting, for fifty cents, on the head of a stalwart negro.—*Mem*. A negro could carry the round earth on his head, if he could only get it there. And here came the discovery of Antonio's vileness,—he had had an eighth of an ounce, wherewith to pay the carriers. According to the bargain, as rehearsed to us, he was to pay them a dollar and three fourths, which would leave him three reals for himself. He professed to have done this with so ingenuous an air, that we were a little ashamed of so small a fee, and added thereto the small remnant of our change. Only at the last moment, when the train was puffing and smoking alongside, did the poor blacks venture to say that one dollar was very little for carrying all those trunks. Our hearts were stirred, but the train was there, the purse empty, and Antonio out of sight. Wherefore, let him, as before said, avoid our second coming.

But there never was a departure without an omission. Something you have forgotten that you meant to take, or you have brought with you something that should have been left. Wending your way from an English mansion of splendid hospitality, a stray towel has found its way into your portmanteau. Before you have discovered this, a confidential letter from the housekeeper overtakes you informing you of the fact, and begging you to return the missing article at once, which you do for six stamps, with a slight tingle in the cheek. In the present instance we have taken nought that was not ours, but we have left an article of domestic dignity and importance.

Stranger, if you should ever sit at that tea-table in the hotel at San Antonio, with the lamp smoking under your nose, and the three tasteless dishes of preserves spread before your sight, a cup of astringent nothingness being offered to you, and a choking stale roll forming the complement of your evening service,—if there and thus you should see a white teapot, with bands of blue, that looks as if it had seen better days, oh then remember us! For we had scarcely settled ourselves in the cars, when a pensive recollection came over us. It was too late to do anything,—we only touched the shoulder of our friend, who was as usual intent upon palms and scenery, and remarked, with a look of melancholy intelligence, "The Teapot is left behind!"

CHAPTER XVIII.

SLAVERY—CUBAN SLAVE LAWS, INSTITUTIONS, ETC.

IT is not with pleasure that we approach this question, sacred to the pugilism of debate. Nor is it worth while to add one word to the past infinity of talk about it, unless that word could have the weight of a new wisdom. We Americans, caught by the revolutionary spirit of the French, make them too much our models, and run too much to grandiloquent speech, and fine moral attitudinizing. The attitudes do not move the world,—the words do not change the intrinsic bearings of things. They whom we attack, the fight being over, sit down and wipe the dust from their faces,—we sit and wipe the sweat from ours,—something stronger than their will or ours passes between us,—it is the great moral necessity which expresses the will of God. We and they are two forces, pulling in opposite ways to preserve the equilibrium of a third point, which we do not see. We must keep to our pulling, they cannot relinquish theirs. The point of solution that shall reconcile and supersede the differences is not in sight, nor has the wisest of us known how to indicate it. Meanwhile, the calm satisfaction with which some of us divide our national moral inheritance, giving them all the vices, and ourselves all the virtues, is at once mournful and ridiculous. Why are we New Englanders so *naïve* as not to see this? When the representative of a handful of men rises to speak, and, alluding to the progress which a great question has made in twenty years, says: "This is all our doing,—behold our work and admire it!" we cannot, but pause and wonder if merely that irruption of bitter words can have produced so sweet a fruit. In this view, what becomes of the moral evolution of the ages, of the slow, sure help of Time, showing new aspects, presenting new possibilities? What becomes of human modesty, which is nearly related to human justice?

I preface with these remarks, because, looking down from where I sit, I cannot curse the pleasant Southern land, nor those who dwell in it. Nor would I do so if I thought tenfold more ill of its corruptions. Were half my body gangrened, I would not smite nor reproach it, but seek with patience an available remedy. This is the half of our body, and the moral blood which brings the evil runs as much in our veins as in theirs.

Looking at realities and their indications, we see a future for the African race, educated by the enslavement which must gradually ameliorate, and slowly die out. We see that in countries where the black men are many, and the white few, the white will one day disappear, and the black govern. In South Carolina, for example, the tide of emigration has carried westward the flower of the white population. In Charleston, all the aristocratic families have their mulatto representatives, who bear their names. There are Pinckneys, Pringles, Middletons, and so on, of various shades of admixture, living in freedom, and forming a community by themselves. There are even mulatto representatives of extinct families, who alone keep from oblivion names which were once thought honorable. These things are indications of changes which will work themselves slowly. Noble efforts have hemmed the evil in, and the great soul of the World watches, we believe, at the borders, and will not suffer the sad contagion to creep over them into the virgin territories. But where the Institution sits at home, with its roots undergrowing the foundations of society, we may be sad, but we must be patient. The enfranchisement of a race, where it is lasting, is always accomplished by the slow and solid progress of the race itself. The stronger people rarely gives Freedom to the weaker as a boon,—when they are able, they rise up and take it with their own hands. It is an earning, not a gift, nor can the attributes which make liberty virtual and valuable be commanded, save under certain moral conditions. A man is not noble because he is free, but noble men constituting a nation become free. Let the wounds of Africa first be stopped,—let her lifeblood stay to enrich her own veins. The enslaved population of Cuba and our own South must, under ordinary circumstances, attain in time a condition in which Slavery shall be impossible.

But our business is with what actually exists. We will leave what shall and should be to the Theorists who invent it, and to God who executes it, often strangely unmindful of their suggestions.

The black and white races are, by all accounts, more mingled in Cuba, than in any part of our own country. People who have long been resident there assure us that some of the wealthiest and most important families are of mixed blood. Animadvert upon this as you will, it is nevertheless certain that it weaves close bonds of affinity between them, and ties of Nature which, though ignored, cannot be unfelt. I have not seen in Cuba anything that corresponds to our ideal separation of the two sets of human beings, living in distinctness one from the other, hating and wronging each other with the fierceness of enemies in the death-grapple. The Negro cannot be so hated, so despised,—it is not in the nature of things. His *bonhommie*, his gentle and attachable nature do not allow it. Nor can he, in return, so hate. There is a great familiarity between the children of the two races. They play, and run about, and are petted together. We made a visit at a Creole house, where the youngest child, a feeble infant of six months, was suckled by a black nurse. "You must see the nurse's Baby," they all said, and the little daughter of the house ran to fetch her, and soon returned, bringing her by one arm, the way in which their own mothers carry them. She was an uncommonly handsome infant, scarcely older than her white foster-brother, but greatly in advance of him in her powers of locomotion. She was, according to custom, entirely naked, but her shining black skin seemed to clothe her, and her fine back and perfect limbs showed that she throve in nudity. She ran about on all fours like some strange creature, so swift and strong was she, and meeting with a chair, pulled herself up by it, and stood dancing on one foot, holding out the other. The family all gathered round her, admiring her color and her shape, and the little girl finally carried her off in triumph, as she had brought her.

The slave children wear oftenest no clothing until five or six years old. They look well-fed and healthy, only the prevalence of umbilical Hernia shows a neglect of proper bandaging at birth,—the same trouble from the same cause is very observable in the south of Italy. The increase of the slaves is, of course, an important test of their treatment,—it is small throughout the Island, and amounts to little save on the best plantations. There is now a slow improvement in this respect. The repression of the slave-trade has caused such a rise in the price of negroes, that it is become better economy to preserve and transmit their lives than to work them off in eight or ten years, leaving no posterity to supply their place. Vile as these motives seem, they are too near akin to the general springs of human action for us to contemn them. Is it otherwise with operatives in England, or with laborers in Ireland? Emigration lessens their numbers, and raises their value,—it becomes important to society that they shall be fed and sustained. One wrong does not excuse another, but where a class of wrongs is universal, it shows a want of moral power in the race, at which the individual cannot justly carp.

Even the race of Coolies, hired at small wages for eight years, and exploitered for that time with murderous severity, have found a suicidal remedy that nearly touches their selfish masters. So many of them emancipated themselves from hard service by voluntary death, that it became matter of necessity to lighten the weight about their necks, and to leave them that minimum of well-being which is necessary to keep up the love of life. The instinct itself is shown to be feeble in the race, whereas the Negro clings to life under whatever pains and torment. The Coolies are valued for their superior skill and intelligence, but as men will treat a hired horse worse than a horse of their own, so they were, until they happily bethought them of killing themselves, more hardly used than the Negroes. Would that horses in the North had the same resource. If the wretched beast, harnessed, loaded, and beaten over the face and head by some greater brute in human shape, could only "his quietus make" by himself, and be found hanging in his stall, what a revolution would there be in the ideas of Omnibus-drivers and Carmen! Self-assassination is, surely, the most available alleviation of despotism. When Death is no longer terrible to the Enslaved, then let the Enslaver look to it.

True, we have heard of horrible places in the interior of the Island, where the crack of the whip pauses only during four hours in the twenty-four, where, so to speak, the sugar smells of the blood of the slaves. We have heard of plantations whereon there are no women, where the wretched laborers have not the privileges of beasts, but are only human machines, worked and watched. There, not even the mutilated semblance of family ties and domestic surroundings alleviates the sore strain upon life and limb. How can human creatures endure, how inflict this? Let God remember them, as we do in our hearts, with tears and supplication.

We have seen too, here and there, fiendish faces which looked as if cruelty and hardness might be familiar to them. The past history of Spain shows to what a point that nation can carry insensibility to the torment of others. Yet the Creoles seem generally an amiable set of people, enduring from the Spanish government much more than they in turn inflict on those beneath them. Nor can we believe that even the Spaniard can be a more dreaded tyrant than the Yankee, where the strong nature of the latter has been left coarse and uncultured, or brutalized by indulgence in vice. The nervous energy of his race makes him a worse demon than the other, while the peaceable and pious traditions of his youth, turned against him, urge him yet further from the sphere of all that is Christian.

The slave laws of Cuba are far more humane than our own. It is only to be doubted whether the magistrates in general are trustworthy in carrying them out. Still, it is the policy of the Government to favor the Negroes, and allow them definite existence as a third class, which would be likely to range with the Government in case of civil war. It is affirmed and believed by the Cubans that the colonial President has in his hands orders to loose the slaves throughout the Island, at the first symptoms of rebellion, that they may turn all their old rancors against their late masters. The humane clauses of which we speak are the following:—

In the first place, every slave is allowed by law to purchase his own freedom, when he has amassed a sum sufficient for the purchase. He can moreover compel his master to receive a small sum in part payment, and then, hiring himself out, can pay the residue from his wages. The law intervenes also, if desired, to fix the price of the slave, which it will reduce to the minimum value. Every slave has the right to purchase his child before birth for the sum of thirty dollars, a fortnight after, for fifty, and so on, the value of course rising rapidly with the age of the child. Again, a slave who complains of ill-treatment on the part of his master may demand to be sold to another, and a limited space of time is allowed, during which he can exert himself to find a purchaser. These statutes do not seem to contemplate the perpetuity of slavery as do our own institutions. What a thrill of joy would run through our Southern and South-Western states, if every slave father and mother had the power to purchase their own offspring for a sum not altogether beyond their reach. How would they toil and starve to accumulate that sum, and how many charitable friends would invest the price of a dress or shawl in such black jewels, which would be the glory of so many black mothers. On the other hand, it is to be feared that the ignorance and poverty of the slaves may, in many places, make the benevolent intention of these statutes null and void. Official corruption, too, may impede their operation. In many parts of our own South, superior enlightenment and a more humane state of public feeling may do something to counterbalance the inferiority of legislation. Still, Americans should feel a pang in acknowledging that even in the dark article of slave laws they are surpassed by a nation which they contemn. Slaves are not sold by public auction, in Cuba, but by private sale. Nor are they subject to such rudeness and insult as they often receive from the lower whites of our own Southern cities. The question now rises, whether in case of a possible future possession of the Island by Americans, the condition of the blacks would be improved. There is little reason to think so, in any case, as our own unmitigated despotism would be enforced; but if their new masters were of the Filibuster type, they might indeed sing with sorrow the dirge of the Creole occupation, and betake themselves to the Coolie expedient of obtaining freedom at small cost.

Not in such familiarity live the Creoles and Spaniards. Here, the attitudes are sharply defined. Oppression on the one hand and endurance on the other appear in a tangible form, and the oppression is conscious, and the endurance compulsory. The Spanish race is in the saddle, and rides the Creole, its derivative, with hands reeking with plunder. Not content with taxes, customs, and prohibitions, all of which pass the bounds of robbery, the Home Government looses on the Colony a set of Officials, who are expected to live by peculation, their salaries being almost nominal, their perquisites, whatever they can get. All State-offices are filled by Spaniards, and even Judgeships and Professorates are generally reserved to them. A man receives an appointment of which the salary may be a thousand dollars per annum. He hires at once an expensive house, sets up a *volante*, dresses his wife and daughters without economy, lives in short at the rate of ten times that sum, and retires after some years, with a handsome competency. What is the secret of all this? Plunder,—twofold plunder, of the inhabitants, and of the Home Government. And this, from the lowest to the highest, is the universal rule. We spoke of customs and prohibitions. Among the first, that on flour seems the most monstrous imposition. No bread-stuffs being raised on the Island, the importation of them becomes almost a condition of life, yet every barrel of wheaten flour from the States pays a duty of eight dollars, so that it becomes cheaper to ship the flour to Spain, and re-ship it thence to Cuba, than to send it direct from here. Of prohibitions, the most striking is that laid upon the vine, which flourishes throughout the Island. It may be cultivated for fruit, but wine must on no account be made from the grape, lest it should spoil the market for the Spanish wines. Among taxes, none will astonish Americans more than the stamp-tax, which requires all merchants, dealers, and bankers to have every page of their books stamped, at high cost. Of course, no business contracts are valid, recorded on any other than stamped paper. To these grievances are added monopolies. All the fish caught on the Island is held at the disposition of Señor Marti, the *Empresario* of the Tacon theatre. This man was once a pirate of formidable character,—after some negotiation with the Tacon Government, he gave up his comrades to justice, receiving in return his own safety, and the monopoly of the fish-market. The price of this article of food is therefore kept at twenty-five cents a pound. These compromises are by no means uncommon. The public Executioner of Havana is a Negro whose life, once forfeit to the State, was redeemed only by his consenting to perform this function for life. He is allowed only the liberty of the Prison. One of our party, visiting that Institution, found this man apparently on the most amicable terms with all the inmates. The *Garrote* being shown, he was asked if it was he who garroted Lopez, and replied in the affirmative, with a grin. Our friend inquired of him how many he had garroted: "How can one tell?" he said, shrugging his shoulders, "so many, so many!" The prisoners chatted and smoked with him, patting him on the back,—making thus that discrimination between the man and his office which is at the bottom of all human institutions. Of the great sums of money received by the Government through direct and indirect taxation, little or nothing revisits the people in the shape of improvements. The Government does not make roads, nor establish schools, nor reform criminals, nor stretch out its strong arm to prevent the offences of ignorant and depraved youth. The roads, consequently, are few and dangerous,—a great part of the Island being traversable only on horseback. There is little or no instruction provided for the children of the poorer classes, and the prisons are abominable with filth, nakedness, and disorder of every kind. There is the same espionage, the same power of arbitrary imprisonment as in Austria, Rome, and Naples, only they have America near them, and in that neighborhood is fear to some, and hope to others. The administration of justice would seem to be one of the worst of all the social plagues that abide in the Island. Nowhere in the world have people a more wholesome terror of going to law. The Government pays for no forms of legal procedure, and a man once engaged in a civil or criminal suit, is at the mercy of Judges and Lawyers who plunder him at will, and without redress. If a man is robbed, the Police come to him at once with offers of assistance and detection. It is often the case that he denies and persists in denying the robbery, rather than be involved in the torment of a suit. Much of what we narrate was common to all the civilized world, an hundred years ago, but the Cubans do not deserve to be held under the weight of these ancient abuses. They are not an effete people, but have something of the spring of the present time in them, and would gladly march to the measure of the nineteenth century, were it not for the decrepit Government whose hand has stiffened with their chains in it. The portrait of the vulgar Queen hangs in nearly every place of note,—she is generally painted at full length, in a blue dress. So coarse and weak is her face that one would think those interested would keep it out of sight, that the abstract idea of royalty might not be lowered by so unqueenly a representation. But this is unjust, for what crowned head of the present day is there that has anything intrinsically august in its aspect?

The Cubans, considered in comparison with the Spaniards, form quite as distinct a people as the Americans, compared with the English. Climate and the habits of insular life have partly brought about this difference, but it has also a moral cause,—a separate interest makes a separate people. The mother-countries that would keep their colonies unweaned must be good nurses. The intermingling of the black element in the Creole race is, as I have said, strongly insisted upon by competent judges,—it is evidently not purely Caucasian, and there seems to be little reason for supposing that it perpetuates any aboriginal descent. The complexion, and in some degree the tastes of these people give some color to the hypothesis of their indebtedness to the African race. The prevailing color of the Creole is not the clear olive of the Spaniard, nor the white of the Saxon,—it is an indescribable, clouded hue, neither fair nor brown. We have seen children at a school who were decidedly dark, and would have been taken for mulattoes in the North,— they had straight hair, vivacious eyes, and coffee-colored skins,—those whom we interrogated called them "*Criollos*" as if the word had a distinct meaning. We could not ascertain that they were considered to be of black descent, though the fact seemed patent. In this school, which we saw at recess only, some of the mischievous boys amused themselves with dragging their comrades up to us, and saying: "Señora, this boy is a mulatto." The accused laughed, kicked, and disclaimed.

The taste of the Cubans, if judged by the European standard, is bad taste. They love noisy music,—their architecture consults only the exigencies of the climate, and does not deserve the name of an art. Of painting they must have little knowledge, if one may judge by the vile daubs which deface their walls, and which would hardly pass current in the poorest New England village. As to dress; although I have whispered for your good, my lady friends, that the most beautiful summer-dresses in the world may be bought in Havana, yet the Creole ladies themselves have in general but glaring and barbaric ideas of adornment, and their *volante*-toilette would give a Parisienne the ague.

The Creoles then, as a race, do not incline to plastic art, nor to the energetic elegancies of life. Theirs is not the nature to grapple with marble or bronze, or with the more intellectual obstacles of Painting. One art remains to them, common to all early civilizations, first in history, first too in rank,—they are Poets. Not only is a facility for versification common amongst them, but they have some names which the real halo adorns. Of these, Heredia, Placido, and Milanés are best known.

This seems a very natural manifestation in their case. Held in check by the despotism of the tropical sun, and excluded from social and political action by the more barbarous despotism of Spain, their minds are turned inward, and their energies flow in the channel of contemplation. For Poetry is the freedom of the oppressed,—it is one voice leaping up where a thousand arms are chained, but the thousand hear it, and take courage. In the dreamy tropical life, the beautiful surroundings must bear some fruit. Those glorious growths of tree and flower, those prickly hedges with the sudden glare of a red sword among them, those inconceivable sunsets and nights without parallel,—these things must all write themselves upon the sensitive Southern nature, and the language in which they write themselves is poetry. How far a wider sphere of action may develop in them more hardy and varied powers is a question not to be solved in the existing state of things.

It does not seem likely that the Cubans will ever by their own act abolish slavery. The indolence and mechanical ineptitude which enter into their characters will make them always a people to be waited on. Perhaps no nation, living below a certain parallel, would be capable of such a deed. The far-off English, in their cool island, could emancipate the slaves in their own Indies, but the English dwelling among them would never have relinquished the welcome service; nor is it likely that the men of our own far South will ever conceive as possible another social *status* than the present relations between master and slave. From the North the impulse must come, and however clogged and sanded with unutterable nonsense of self-gratulation and vituperation of the brother man, we must welcome it. The enslaved race too, gradually conquering the finer arts of its masters, will rise up to meet the hand of deliverance, having in due course of time reached that spiritual level at which enslavement becomes impossible.

Sismondi, in the second volume of his Essays, has some sensible remarks on the farming system as pursued in Tuscany, where the farmer is employed on long leases, receiving one half the profits of the farm worked by him. Sismondi sufficiently sets forth the advantages of this over all other systems of leasing and underletting, as it allows the husbandman a well-being in direct proportion to the thoroughness and persistency of his labors. After speaking of the apparent failure of English emancipation, he ascribes the idleness of the freed blacks to their entire want of interest in the landed property about them, and proposes associating them in this way to the interests of their would-be employers. For the world can hardly afford that these people should merely feed and grovel in the sun, when all the tillage of the tropics lies fitted to their hand. Nor will it much longer afford, let us hope, that the human tool shall work without the advantage that individual will and interest alone can give him. They who thus consent to use the man without his crowning faculties are like those who would purchase the watch without the main-spring.

How all this is to end, doth not yet appear. The abstract principles of right and wrong we know, but not the processes, nor the duration of their working out in history. All the white handkerchiefs in Exeter Hall will not force the general Congress of Nations to decide questions otherwise than by the laws of convenience and advantage. England as a power has never lifted a finger nor a breath against Russian serfdom or Austrian oppression; and the Spanish government she is determined to uphold in Cuba is reeking with abominations of which she cannot afford to be cognizant.

I know that God has in His power swift miracles of redemption. He can command the sudden Exodus of a wronged people, and can raise bloody waves of wrath over the heads of their oppressors. But we cannot call down these wonders, nor foretell their appointed time. Meantime, the ram's horn Fantasias which our modern Prophets have so long been performing against the walls of the southern Jericho do not seem to have had the Divine commission to overthrow them.

I feel that any one in the North who gives a mild, perhaps palliative view of slavery, will be subject to bitter and severe censure. But this should surely make no difference to us in the sincere and simple statement of our impressions. Intellectual justice revolts from the rhetorical strainings, exaggerations, and denaturalizations of facts which the Partisan continually employs, but which the Philosopher and Historian must alike reject. Moral justice dissents from the habitual sneer, denunciation, and malediction, which have become consecrated forms of piety in speaking of the South. Believe me, in so far as we allow personal temper, spite, or uncharity, place in our treatment of a holy cause, in so far we do it wrong. Believe me, too, that the actual alleviations which often temper the greatest social evils should not be left out of sight, lest an atheistic despair should settle on the minds of men. The overruling mercy of God is everywhere,—in the North and in the South it has its work of consolation and of compensation. It absolves us from no possible reform, from no labor for the amelioration of the condition of our fellow-men. But as it limits alike the infliction and endurance of wrong, and sets bounds which the boldest and wickedest dare not pass, we must not paint the picture of what is, without it.

So, with thoughts reverting to the slow and mighty operations in the World of Nature, which seem to have their counterpart in the World of Life and Fate,—trusting in the wisdom of the gray-haired centuries, even when the half-grown ones call them Fool, I finish my Chapter of philosophizing, somewhat, no doubt, to the relief of my Reader, but very much more to my own.

CHAPTER XIX.

FAREWELL!

FAREWELL to Havana! the pleasant time is over. We are to return where we belong. Not with undue sentimentalism of sorrow, as though it were greater loss to see beautiful places and forsake them, than to have staid at Pudding-gut Point, Coxackie, or Martha's Vineyard all one's life, having beheld and regretted nothing else. When travellers tear themselves from the maternal bosom of Rome, a pang is inevitable, and its expression allowable. Even meretricious Paris sometimes harpoons an honest American heart more deeply than is fit. But there are those, born and bred amongst us, who return from their foreign travel with wide-mouthed lamentation over the past enjoyment. Others snippingly accost one with: "I cannot bear your climate,"——. "Strange," I reply, "since it bore you." We are not so deeply moved at leaving Havana, though to go to sea is always as unnatural an act as having a tooth pulled. The green earth reminds us that it is our element, and the slowly counted palms nod to us: "Remember,—remember!" We indulge ourselves in a last drive, and take kind farewell of the gay streets, the Plaza, the Paseo, and the Cerro, with its blue villas and palm-bordered gardens. Beautiful those gardens are in their own way,—Nature refusing to be kept down, but excusing her irregularities by their wild and graceful results. There is Count Fernandino's garden,—we have not described that, have we? Palms, flowers, fruit-trees, a marble pavilion with a marble Venus, a bath-house painted in fresco, paved with fine tiling, and lit through stained glass, an ethereal trellis and canopy of fairy-like iron-work, painted coral-red, and hung with vines, whose industry in weaving themselves is almost perceptible to the eye,—still, shady walks, and evermore palms. We passed a morning there with some botanical friends, and had much explained to us that we cannot possibly remember. This we did retain, that there are known on the island sixty varieties of palms, and that this garden contains at least forty of them.

And here is Doña Herrera's garden, which we visited one morning, with our friends of the Cup of Tea, (*vide* earlier letters). How soft and dewy was it in the morning light! the flowers had still the dreamy starlight in them. We ran about like children, admiring at every moment something new and strange. In the middle of the garden was a fairy lake, with a little mock steamboat upon it, the paddles being moved by hand. There were gas fixtures disposed throughout the grounds, which are lighted on the occasion of a *fête champêtre*. What a time the young people must have of it, then! There is an Aviary, too, with the remnant of a collection of tropical birds, and a small Menagerie, with a fox, a monkey, and a 'coon. We ask permission to see the house, and our friends having sent in their good names, Doña Maria walks slowly out to meet us. She is a plain, elderly woman, short and stout, with a pleasant voice and gentle manners. She has rather a splendid nest, for a bird of such sober plumage, but all its adornments are in good taste. She shows us first a cool Banqueting-room, where the table is invitingly laid for her Ladyship's own breakfast,—it is painted in fresco, and opens on the garden,—then come the Drawing-rooms, then an exquisite Bedroom hung with blue, the bed and mosquito-netting being adorned with rich lace, then a Picture-gallery, which serves as an Oratory, a cabinet in the wall containing and concealing the altar. Then comes a small room, adorned by her Ladyship's own hands, with paper flowers and stuffed birds, lighted by a pretty, tiny glass dome, and then, endless thanks, good Doña Maria, and farewell forever. For as I love not stuffed birds, nor paper flowers, no, nor mass neither, it is not likely that I shall bear your Ladyship company in Heaven, even should both of us get there, which, while we continue to live and sin, must be considered as uncertain.

Other visions unroll themselves as we review our Havana days and ways. Our voyage up the spire of the Cathedral, with swimming eyes and dizzy head. Our friends go bravely through it, and ascend even the last little rickety wooden staircase, calling back for us as the chimney-sweeper sings out from the top of the chimney. Where is Hulia? holding on to a beam with frantic eagerness, deaf to entreaty and encouragement. She is persuaded at last to relinquish it, and is hoisted, pushed, and dragged to the top where, opening her unwilling eyes, she seeks the first strong point of masonry, and hugs it, admiring the view in convulsive sentences, as occasion demands. The point is tolerably lofty, and the view extensive, but one loses many of its beauties in looking down from such an elevation. We must remember this, and not ascribe to St. Simeon Stylites too great an advantage in the enjoyment of natural scenery. Then, after the perilous descent, our exploration of the Cathedral itself, with its shrine of porphyry, and little other adornment,—the pious thoughtfulness of the Sacristan, who, when we pass the host, tells us that "His Majesty is there," and his look of amazement when we do not bow or bend the knee at this intelligence. Then, that refreshing season in the Sacristy, with a graceless young Sub-Deacon, intent upon extending to us all the hospitalities of the church. "Here is the incense,"—he burns some of it under our nostrils; "here is the wine for the Sacrament,—taste of it," and he pours out a tolerable portion, and, handing it to us to sip, tosses off the residue with a smack. "Here is the oil and salt for baptism,—you won't like that, but you may taste it if you choose." And then, he tumbles over all the priest's garments. "This crimson brocade is for high feasts,—this green for common occasions,—this black velvet for funerals,—this white scarf is for marriages." You really begin to regard the Priest as a sort of chameleon, whose color changes with the spiritual food he lives on. Rascal-neophyte, you will be as sanctimonious as the priest himself some day, and as sincere.

But all this is in the past, and we have got really to our last of Havana. The last purchases have been made; by great economy we have accomplished a little extravagance. The farewell visits have been paid,—we have paid also the necessary four dollars for the privilege of leaving the Island. Copious leave-takings follow, between ourselves and our long companions at the Hotel,—follow the Bill and servants' fees,—and then, having been waked after a short night's rest, there remains no further excuse for our not taking the boat at early morning, and delivering ourselves into their hands who are to return us to our native country.

So, Havana is done with. We are sad and sorry to leave it, but do not sentimentalize, recalling Sheridan's sensible lines:—

"Oh, matchless excellence! and must we part?

Well, if we must, we must, and in that case,

The less is said, the better."

There is a large party of us known to each other in our late wanderings; and as we meet on board, we make a tolerable attempt at cheerfulness. But the thought of the Northern cold lies heavy upon every heart, for though it is late in March, we know where the east wind is now, and will be for two months to come. We are soon in motion, and, casting a last look towards our sky-blue hotel, we see some of the Almy-ites waving flags of truce at us. We seize whatever is at hand, and make the usual frantic demonstrations. Farewell, Morro Castle! farewell, Isla de Cuba! We have nothing left us now but the Steamer. This is the Isabel, greatly be-puffed in the Charleston papers, but rarely praised, one should think, by those who have been in her. Breakfast is served us in a cabin without ventilation, where to breathe is disgusting, to eat, impossible. We explore our state-room,—the thermometer stands at 100° in it, but the day is hot, and we do not suspect any other reason for its high temperature. From these dens we emerge as quickly as possible to the open air, and get ourselves on deck. The Southern seas are always detestable; and though there is no wind to speak of, it soon gets rough, and people stiffen in their places, and go to sleep, or go below, and are never heard of more. Dinner is eaten mostly on the upper deck, but the demand is not large. Iced champagne proves a friend in need. We reach Key West early in the afternoon. The landing is ugly, and though we stop an hour or more, we are expressly told "ten minutes," in order that the Captain may not be bothered with our going on shore. We have here a last look at the cocoa-palm, which grows along the coast. White sea-corals are brought for sale; many turtles are taken on board and laid on their backs, their fins being tied together; also, an invalid in a chair, in the last stages of decline. The turtles remain, for the fifty-six hours that follow, helpless and untended. So piteous do they seem, that one of us suggests "the last sigh of the turtle" as a commemorative title for the aromatic soup that is to follow.

And this is all of Key West. On going below at bed-time, our bare feet find the floor of the state-room scorching hot. On inquiry, we find ourselves directly over the boiler,—a pleasant situation in an American steamer. We consider ourselves nearer translation than ever before, and go to sleep trying to show just reason why we should not be blown up, as better people have been, before morning.

Next morning—Oh let me here breathe a word of advice to those who plough the Southern seas. Rise early in the morning, if you mean to rise at all, for the sea is quietest then, before the wind is up; and if you are once dressed and on deck, you have a chance. Next morning none were able to get up who were not up by six o'clock,—for by that time the day's work was begun, and people only staid and stiffened where they were. Now do not fear, I have described sea-sickness once and for all; this paper shall not be nauseous with new details. But for love of the dear old Karnak, I must show up this pinchbeck Isabel; this dirty, disorderly floating prison, where no kind care alleviated one's miseries, and no suitable diet helped one's recovery. On board the Karnak, Steward, Stewardess, and Captain followed you up with the zeal of loving-kindness. Here, the hateful black servants flit past you like a dream. If you try to detain them, they vanish with a grin, and promising to return, take care to avoid you in future. N. B.—I call them hateful, because of the true American steam-boat breed, smirking, supercilious, and unserviceable. There, mattresses and cushions were plentifully supplied, and you might lie on deck, if you could not sit up. Here, not even a pillow could be brought. You sit all day bolt upright in a miserable wooden chair, holding your aching head first with this hand, now with that, and wondering that your suffering body can hold together so long. There, the log, the daily observation, the boatswain's whistle, the pleasant bells ringing the hour. Here, no log, no observation, no boatswain, no bells. There, in a word, comfort and confidence; here, distrust and disgust. But we drop the parallel.

To us, that dark day was as a vision of familiar faces, strangely distorted and discolored, of friends, usually kind and attentive, who sit grimly around, and looking on one's misery, do not stir to help it. There is a pillow, ah! if somebody would only lay it under this heavy head, that cannot be held up by the weary hand any longer. Henry there is going to do it,—he has got the pillow,—no, he puts it under his own head, regarding me with the glare of a sickly cannibal. One good creature flings half of her blanket over my shivering knees. I know not her name, nor her nature, but I know that she is blessed, and worthy of Paradise. Going below for a moment, I pass through the after-cabin, and see such a collection of wretches as would furnish forth a Chamber of Horrors to repletion. With tossed clothes, disordered hair, and wild eyes, they lie panting for air, which they don't get. We are better off upstairs, and I return to my wooden chair and end of a blanket, with enthusiasm. But the day passes, and at night we are down again in the state-room over the boiler, with the ports screwed up, and no air to temper the heat. No matter, our weary skeleton refuses to be kept upright any more,—we lie and sleep. And at two in the morning, one of the strong-minded, who could not sleep, arose, and found that the sea was down, and that the ports might be opened, only that the man who had charge of them was asleep. Wherefore she aroused the slumbering traitor with the wholesome clarion of a woman's tongue, and he got up and fumbled about till he found the port-wrench, wherewith he unscrewed all the ports, and we took heart, and revived. The next day was all smooth sailing,—we ate our victuals on deck, and were thankful. And that evening, say at six o'clock, we made the welcome port of Charleston, and went on shore, hoping never to leave it more.

Let me not forget to say that at the last moment, when all possibility of service was over, the faithless blacks came about us, and were full of hopes that we were better, smiling and lingering very much as if they expected a fee. But if any of us were weak enough to comply with their desires, for the honor of human nature suffer me to draw a veil over such base compliance, and let the World think they got only what they deserved, which is little enough in any case, and in theirs, nothing.

And now, Reader, if I have one, farewell. The Preacher who speaks even to one, has his congregation before him, but the poor Scribbler is left to his own illusions, and calls up for himself a gorgeous Public, where perhaps he has only himself for company. Still, it is safest to imagine a Public; and having imagined one, I here take a kind leave of it. If any have followed me along in my travels, and wished me God-speed, I hereby thank them heartily. If any have treated with discourtesy a true word here and there which does not tally with their own notions, so much the worse for them, and for any cause which cannot bear sincerity. And so, wishing that you might all see the pleasant things I have described, and thinking that you cannot have been half so weary in reading these pages as I have been in writing them, I will prolong no further the sweet sorrow of parting, only God bless you, and Good-bye.

THE END.

Milton Keynes UK
Ingram Content Group UK Ltd.
UKHW031631231024
450082UK00005B/438